THE PLOT
TO SUBVERT
WARTIME
NEW ZEALAND

HUGH PRICE, born in 1929, left Masterton in 1948 to attend Victoria University, when it comprised just the Hunter and Kirk Buildings and a scattering of prefabs. After graduating with an MA in history he decided to be a book publisher. In London he became a book buyer for Whitcombe and Tombs, took a course in book design at the Camberwell School of Arts, and worked for several publishers including Gollancz and Penguin.

Back in Wellington Hugh managed the radical co-op bookshop, Modern Books, founded Price Milburn publishers with his friend Jim Milburn, and worked as an art editor at School Pubs. In 1963 he became the first manager of Sydney University Press. Five years later he came back to Wellington, and ran Price Milburn. In 1974 the firm earned a coveted Export Award for its school reading books.

As Publishing Consultant to Victoria University from 1970 to 1978, Hugh was instrumental in the founding and early publishing of VUP.

Hugh is married to Beverley Randell, MNZM, the author of many books for fledgling readers. Their daughter is Susan Price, the collector of quality children's books. Together, the family restored the historic Randell Cottage in Thorndon, and gave it to a Trust that runs it as a writers' retreat for New Zealand and French authors.

A brush with the SIS early in the 1950s sparked interest in the subject of security intelligence that is at the heart of *The Plot to Subvert Wartime New Zealand*. Hugh likes to think that publication fulfils the wish of the then Prime Minister, who said, '. . . it is one of the most extraordinary instances of human credulity I have ever heard of in my life . . . I hope the whole story will be written up.'

So here it is at last!

THE PLOT
TO SUBVERT
WARTIME
NEW ZEALAND

A true story of
an impudent hoax
that convulsed New Zealand
in the darkest days of World War II,
and that the Commissioner of Police
declared 'beyond comprehension'

A hoax, moreover, that
expanded to challenge the
rule of law in the Dominion

HUGH PRICE

VICTORIA UNIVERSITY PRESS
WELLINGTON
2006

VICTORIA UNIVERSITY PRESS
Victoria University of Wellington
PO Box 600 Wellington
vuw.ac.nz/vup

National Library of New Zealand Cataloguing-in-Publication Data

Price, Hugh, 1929-
The plot to subvert wartime New Zealand : a true story of an
impudent hoax that convulsed New Zealand in the darkest days
of World War II, and that the Commissioner of Police declared
'beyond comprehension' : a hoax, moreover, that expanded to
challenge the rule of law in the Dominion / Hugh Price.
Includes bibliographical references.
ISBN-13: 978-0-86473-538-6
ISBN-10: 0-86473-538-3
1. Ross, Sydney Gordon, 1909-1946. 2. Impostors and
imposture—New Zealand—History. 3. Intelligence service—
New Zealand—History. 4. World War, 1939-1945—New
Zealand—History. I. Title.
364.163—dc 22

Set in Sabon and Courier, with Trajan and Caslon Openface titling

Printed by Astra Print, Wellington

Contents

Documents

ACKNOWLEDGEMENTS

I thank the New Zealand Security Intelligence Service for making available the interesting historical papers on which this book is based.

I am very grateful for help from the Stout Research Centre, Victoria University of Wellington, which gave collegial support, and made a convenient room available to me to plan this book in. I am grateful, too, to James Traue, whose specialist knowledge tracked down items I could not find myself.

I was greatly helped by Julie Beadle, Syd Ross's great-niece, who supplied documents and oral information about the Ross family.

For editorial help I have had advice from my friend Roger Steele, who caused me to tidy up several tangles and awkward passages. I owe special thanks to my daughter Susan Price and my wife Beverley Randell, both of whom read several drafts of the work and suggested improvements, and gave me a lot of very welcome encouragement along the way.

INTRODUCTION

BEYOND COMPREHENSION

*How an imaginative wartime prank turned into
the country's most astonishing scandal –
with a bizarre twist at its centre*

The story that follows is true, and parts of it have already
been aired many times, and published in several places.
For years after World War II it was in the repertoire of
anyone who enjoyed telling astonishing anecdotes about
wartime New Zealand. Journalists who made a business
of irritating the wartime Prime Minister, Peter Fraser,
and his colourful Minister of Public Works, Bob Semple,
kept recycling the handful of known facts of the case,
and kept the story alive.

The *Auckland Star* was the first in the field with a
long article, 'New Zealand's Greatest Hoax', on page
6 of its issue of 18 September 1944. Then the National
Party's weekly newspaper *Freedom* ran the 'full story of
the Folkes Affair' three times (25.1.50, 4.3.53, 7.8.57)
and *New Zealand Truth* seven times (29.7.42, 3.2.43,
2.10.43, 23.8.44, 19.9.45, 6.11.46, 24.6.80), and the
New Zealand Observer once (13.11.46). The story was
put on the formal historical record when Professor F.L.W.
Wood's 1958 volume of the official war history, *The New
Zealand People at War,* was published (War History
Branch, Department of Internal Affairs), and again in
Nancy M. Taylor's companion war history *The Home
Front* 1986 (Volume II, page 884). In September 1982

7

the *New Zealand Listener* ran a piece by David Filer that added a few new scraps of information. A related half-hour docudrama (TV1, 30.9.82), produced by David Baldock, told the story, with Frank Edwards as Ross, Bernard Kearns as Peter Fraser, and Terry Connolly as Folkes. This programme was broadcast again on TV1 on 18 February 1984.

There the saga seems to have ended, and I have not since then met any newspaper reader who recollects any of those journalistic pieces, nor a single viewer who remembers seeing either TV showing of the docudrama . . . while the generation of raconteurs who used to entertain dining or partying acquaintances with the story has gone. Dramatic events of early 1942 have faded to make way for more recent public excitements and crises. After all, 1942 is about as distant from today as excitements of the Boer War were to us then.

In the late 1980s my friend Professor Wood, who was head of the History Department at Victoria University College in Wellington in the 1940s and 1950s, suggested to me that the story was rich and interesting enough to stand the change from a journalistic set-piece to a researched and carefully written book. He was sorry that he had not turned up much for the war history he had written, but he told me that he was sure that some interesting papers that were not available to him then could now be prised from the New Zealand Security Intelligence Service, with the help of the Official Information Act and, perhaps, a nudge from the Office of the Ombudsman. These documents, he guessed, might throw light on this episode that erupted for the few months when our country stood in peril of invasion, and normal rational discourse was diminished, allowing surprising things to happen that must be amazing – *if not unbelievable* – to younger readers sixty and more years later.

ONE Television New Zealand

Programme schedules are correct at time of publication but subject to later amendment.

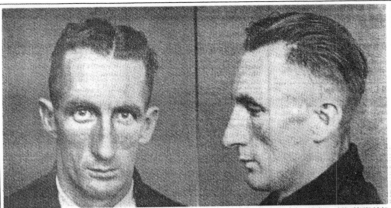

For three months in 1942 this man, **Sydney Gordon Ross**, had the Security Intelligence Bureau, precursor of the SIS, hanging on his every word as he detailed a nationwide spy network paving the way for a Nazi invasion. It was perhaps New Zealand's greatest hoax and its motive was to fulfil every conman's inner desire — to humble the high and mighty. First screened in 1982, the TVNZ documentary **THE ROSS CONSPIRACY** gets a repeat screening tonight at 7.00.

Director LEON THAU
Writer ROGER PRICE
Producer VIC HUGHES
THAMES

4.40 Star Trek

The Doomsday Machine: Kirk goes to the rescue of the starship Constellation which has been virtually destroyed by a huge doomsday machine. He finds only one survivor, Commodore Decker, who elected to remain with his ship. (R) (Final)

Capt James Kirk **William Shatner**
Mr Spock **Leonard Nimoy**
Scotty **James Doohan**
Sulu **George Takei**
Commodore Decker **William Windom**
Lt Palmer **Elizabeth Rogers**
Elliot **John Copage**
Writer NORMAN SPINRAD
Producer GENE COON
Director MARC DANIELS
PARAMOUNT

5.30 Wildtrack

Peter and Margaret take a look on the wild side. This week: A search for the brightest lepidoptera. (R)
Editor PETER HAYDEN
Producer NEIL HARRAWAY
TELEVISION NEW ZEALAND

6.00 M*A*S*H

Quo Vadis, Captain Chandler? An intelligence officer and a psychiatrist are confronted with a wounded officer who says he's Jesus Christ. (R)
Hawkeye **Alan Alda**
Mulcahy **William Christopher**
B.J. **Mike Farrell**
Radar **Gary Burghoff**
Captain Chandler **Alan Fudge**
Colonel Flagg **Edward Winter**

Writer BURT PRELUTSKY
Producer/director GENE REYNOLDS
20TH CENTURY-FOX

6.30 News

TELEVISION NEW ZEALAND

7.00 The Ross Conspiracy

A dramatised documentary telling the true tale of New Zealand's greatest hoax. The year was 1942; the main characters conman Sydney Gordon Ross, Prime Minister Peter Fraser and the head of the Secret Service, Major Kenneth Folkes. Between them they brought down the Security Intelligence Bureau. (R)

Ross **Frank Edwards**
Fraser **Bernard Kearns**
Folkes **Terry Connolly**
Writer/presenter DEREK PAYNE
Researcher DAVID FILER
Producer/director DAVID BALDOCK
TELEVISION NEW ZEALAND

7.30 Coronation Street

How can Eddie Yeats tell his new girlfriend Marion Willis that he is not the tycoon she thinks he is?
GRANADA

8.30 Sport on One Special
XIV WINTER OLYMPIC GAMES

Tonight's coverage centres on the Nordic discipline of ski jumping as well as featuring men's figure skating, women's speed skating and men's cross-country skiing.

Presenters PHILLIP LEISHMAN
ANN-MARIE QUINN
Producer IAIN EGGLETON
TELEVISION NEW ZEALAND

10.30 Summertime Movie
THE AMBUSHERS (1967)

Still trying to stay in retirement from the counter-espionage agency known as ICE, Matt Helm is called in by MacDonald, his former chief. Helm's assignment is to track down an American spacecraft which has been hijacked. (R)

Starring DEAN MARTIN
SANTA BERGER
JANICE RULE
ALBERT SALMI
Writer HERBERT BAKER
Director HENRY LEVIN
COLUMBIA

★ See **Films on TV**, page 97.

12.10 News

TELEVISION NEW ZEALAND

(Closedown at 12.15)

XIV WINTER OLYMPICS: Coverage, 8.30pm.

Television listing for *The Ross Conspiracy*, NZ Listener,
11 February 1984

Here is the single paragraph in Professor Wood's book that comprised all the information he could find on the Folkes Affair:

> . . . In view of the events of 1940 and of the probability that there were some, if very few, people at liberty in New Zealand who would do what they could to harm the country's war effort, it was not surprising that special action should have been taken to strengthen security arrangements. The particular action taken, however, provided an unhappy example of the dangers that attend hasty improvisation in these matters; though, in the first instance at least, the fault does not seem to have lain at the New Zealand end. In November 1940 a representative of the United Kingdom Security Intelligence Organisation transmitted to the New Zealand War Cabinet proposals for the establishment of a security service organisation in New Zealand and 'especially recommended' that a Lieutenant Folkes be lent to New Zealand to control it. Accordingly in February 1941, Folkes, now a major, was appointed as Director of a Security Intelligence Bureau responsible directly to the Prime Minister for civil as well as military security. The Bureau never seems to have functioned satisfactorily. Apart from the circumstances that Major Folkes himself seems to have been unsuited to his responsibilities and that many of his subordinates lacked at least the training necessary for them, War Cabinet does not seem to have appreciated the extent to which the Police Department was already discharging, in an unobtrusive way, the duties projected for the new organisation. The consequence was a duplication of effort, and friction between the SIB and the police. The Security Intelligence Bureau was received with general uneasiness and distrust. It seems to have done a certain amount of useful work in testing and providing security precautions particularly in connection with shipping and wharves, but the suspicion that it was accumulating lurid reports without the inclination to check or the capacity to evaluate

them was confirmed in the most startling fashion in mid-1942. On the 28th of March 1942, the day following his release from Waikeria Reformatory, an individual with an extensive criminal history, including convictions for false pretences, interviewed Mr Semple with a story of having been approached by enemy agents. Semple took him to Fraser, who passed him on to Major Folkes. Over the ensuing three months he seems to have convinced Folkes and, it would appear, some members of the War Cabinet, that four Nazi agents had arrived by submarine and were living in Rotorua, that contacts had been made with fifth columnists throughout the country and plans made for extensive sabotage and the assassination of leading cabinet ministers prior to the landing of an invasion force at New Plymouth. Meanwhile, in pursuit of the conspirators, Folkes's informant, supplied with ample funds by the SIB and accompanied by its agents, toured the North Island. The police were not informed, though from their observation of the individual concerned they began to discover what was happening; nor were the Chiefs of Staff, until, in the closing stages, Folkes asked them for a large body of military personnel in order to round up the conspirators. He also unsuccessfully asked the Prime Minister for special powers, apparently to arrest and detain the considerable number of completely innocent people who had been accused of complicity in the affair. Fraser's suspicions were growing and, some time in July, he requested the police to investigate. They had little difficulty in exposing the affair as a hoax. Despite a devastating report on the work of the Bureau by the Attorney General dated 18 September, and a Chief of Staff paper dated 22 December recommending the immediate dismissal of its head, it was not until 19 February that the Prime Minister wrote directing Folkes to hand over control of his organisation to Mr J. Cummings, then Superintendent of Police. For the remainder of the war the Bureau worked closely with the police and without notoriety.

The Bureau has changed its name twice since then. In 1946 it was transferred to the control of the police and became the Police Special Branch (PSB). About ten years later, PSB – with the files from both organisations – became the New Zealand Security Intelligence Service (SIS), with Brigadier H.E. Gilbert at its head.

On 3 December 1991 I wrote to Lieut. General Don McIvor, then Director of Security and head of the SIS, asking to see the papers that related to the New Zealand career of Major Folkes, and papers on the work of the SIB and perhaps the PSB until February 1947. The response came a few days later, and was encouraging . . . yes, the SIS had some papers about Folkes – and could I be more specific in my requests, please? But for papers on the SIB to February 1947 the answer was no, because some sections of the Official Information Act 1982 raised problems.

The Act includes several sections that give conclusive reasons for withholding official information – particularly if making it available is likely to prejudice the security or defence of New Zealand, or the international relations of the government, or prejudice the entrusting of information to the government of New Zealand by other countries or international organisations. Another reason for withholding is to protect the privacy of persons, and yet another applies if information cannot be made available without a lot of time-consuming and expensive collation and research.

On 22 April I complained to the Ombudsman about this refusal, arguing that my viewing of these wartime papers of the SIB fifty years after the end of World War II could not possibly prejudice the security or defence of New Zealand. I would like to read these historical papers because they might throw an interesting light on public attitudes and events in wartime New Zealand. As for the idea that the information could not be made available to me without a lot of collation and research – well, that sounded pretty thin to me.

The Ombudsman took about a year to respond to my complaint. On 7 April 1993 I had a letter from him telling me that the real trouble was that the files of the SIB were thoroughly mixed with more recent SIS files, and that it would take a lot of work to disentangle them. So – there was a good reason to refuse my request. He regretted that he could not be more helpful.

Well, here was progress. The Ombudsman had disallowed all but one reason for refusing – that it would take an unreasonable time to isolate the papers that I wanted. It was time for me to compromise and limit my request to only those papers that related to the 1942 Folkes affair . . . that could hardly be filed with post-war papers.

With that, and a final flurry of letters, and my payment of $1,100 in photocopying costs, a pile of papers was declassified and released to me. They turned out to be chiefly copies of routine police reports about Syd Ross – the man 'with an extensive criminal history' whom Professor Wood touched on (but did not name) in his war history. There were only a few copies of papers from the SIB, but two of these were letters from Folkes to the Prime Minister, and these were the most interesting of all. Missing was routine correspondence within the SIB, that, we learn from the police files, was accumulated in a series of big scrap-books, commonly called 'the volumes'. Information in these was typed on sheets of paper that were pasted in and carefully indexed – and copied to two identical sets of volumes, one of which was kept by Major Folkes at SIB Headquarters in Wellington, and the other in the Prime Minister's office in Parliament Buildings.

These 'volumes' must have been quite massive, because their bulk was several times remarked on, and late in the story the Police Commissioner reads from 'page 543,

Volume 4', and in Document 1 on page 129 of this book he refers to 'page 595 of Volume 5'.

Unfortunately, none of these big scrapbooks has turned up, which is a pity because they must carry interesting stories – several times knowledgeable officers muttered to the effect that '. . . by golly these volumes will make best sellers when they're published after the war!'

I wonder . . . does any reader of this book happen to know what happened after the war to those compendious volumes – were they binned to help erase details that might help to keep the whole embarrassing story going, or were they thrown out because they were stuffed with false evidence about innocent people? Or are some still lying about? It would be interesting to know.

I have done my best to do justice to this astonishing story, while charting a course between the twin perils of fatigue and obsession. The second of these has been a worry because the story keeps flowing into fresh areas that are full of surprises, and new matters that have not been explored before – such as the nightly work of New Zealand-based radio operators who were part of a world-wide Allied network that was tracking morse-code signals from Nazi U-boats in the Atlantic during World War II. Or what about the patriotic 'whistle blowing' by the New Zealand Communist Party to expose a group that they identified as Nazi-oriented servicemen? Generally I have stuck to my story and not chased too far after these hares.

The Matter of Footnotes

I have decided that regular footnotes to identify sources used in this book are not needed, because the whole story is based on a collection of papers, which (so far as I know) exists in only one set – that I hold. That set was gathered from a wider collection held by the New

Zealand Security Intelligence Service, and kept securely.

To meet these unusual conditions I will deposit the set of papers that I hold in the Beaglehole Room of the Victoria University of Wellington library, in a box labelled *Ross hoax / Folkes affair, 1940s*, where it may be consulted by researchers, and, at the discretion of the Librarian, anyone with a mind to do so.

As it happens, the text of my book verifies itself, as the final pages comprise reports that were written at the time by senior public servants such as the Attorney General and the Commissioner of Police. Both were asked by Cabinet, or the Prime Minister, to set out on paper *what had happened*. This they do, in the appended *Documents*, with suitable expostulations of incredulity.

Other *Documents* are gathered from an item published in a journal, and from news items in mainstream newspapers. These are clearly sourced so that they can be easily found.

H.P.

CHAPTER 1

RELEASE FROM PRISON

Syd Ross was released from Waikeria prison on Saturday 28 March 1942. Waikeria is an isolated dot at the centre of the map of the North Island of New Zealand, just seven miles (about 11 km) from Te Awamutu. He was due for release in the morning. If matters took the usual course remembered by other prisoners, he would have reported to the Governor's door after breakfast, dressed in slacks and jacket, with a worn suitcase secured by a leather strap, and a coat over his arm. The Governor would have counted out a few pounds due to him, and then slipped into his 'You fellas never cease to amaze me . . .' line of thought as he leafed through a file of varied papers under a cover sheet headed 'Ross, S.G.' over a list of *Police Gazette* references and a pasted-down photo.

'Yeah, here we are . . . jeez, *over a dozen* convictions . . . starting in 1930 I see . . . believe me fella, the cops are on to you . . . look, you've got your photo in the old *Gazette* twice, and so far apart that your hair's thinned out between them. Anyway, think hard before you fall to temptation my friend . . . mind you, we can always find you a bunk back here you know . . .'

'Okay, I'll keep it in mind if I'm passing the gate' – an easy promise as the prison was at the end of its own road. A fumbled handshake and Ross would have let himself out of the front door and scrunched across the gravel path, pulled on his coat, and climbed into the service van that would take him to the railway station at Te Awamutu, in time to catch the 11 a.m. train to Frankton Junction.

Ross fished his rail pass from his breast pocket and firmly crossed out the AK that would have taken him to Auckland and his home in Ellerslie. He printed WN instead, adding a squiggle that could have been a validating initial.

Later that night he clambered, stiff and cold, into a dim but warm carriage of the overnight Auckland to Wellington train, accommodation once called by a poet 'a hovel on wheels', and settled himself on to an unyielding leather seat. Other passengers would have been there, sprawled inelegantly, trying to catch a little sleep.

After a while, a blast on a distant steam whistle and a clang on the station bell and some shouts of railway argot, and the train was on its way through thinly settled stretches of dark country . . . to Wellington. As Ross settles down for the discomforts and indignities of second-class long distance rail travel in 1942 New Zealand, we have time to explore this man who will soon be at the centre of a quite astounding episode.

Sydney Gordon Ross, sometimes called Sydney George Ross, but more commonly Syd Ross, was born in Thames on 6 February 1909, the son of a blacksmith, Charles Godfrey Ross, and his wife, Maretta Elizabeth Ross. He attended Waiokaraka School from 1915 to 1918 and then moved with his family to Otahuhu, and then on to Onehunga. The *Dictionary of New Zealand Biography*, Volume Five, describes him as a tall, slim man with light brown hair and a long sharp nose. In the late 1920s he held down some labouring jobs, with stints as an electrician, baker and salesman.

After that, and perhaps because of the economic crash of 1929, things took another turn as Syd Ross accumulated many criminal convictions, mainly for safe-breaking, theft, burglary, trespass, receiving stolen goods and false pretences – all crimes of insolence, not violence. Some of the misdemeanours had an element of theatre

Copy of criminal record listed in the Police Gazette
MC = Magistrates Court SC = Supreme Court

Ross, Sidney George *alias* Ross, Sydney Gordon

Born 1910, **Height** 5ft 11in   Fresh complexion, brown hair, grey eyes.
Labourer / baker / electrician
Died 6 November 1946

Onehunga MC	6.3.30	False pretences (2 charges)	2 years probation
Auckland MC	18.7.30	Theft	2 years in Borstal
Auckland SC	6.7.32	Uttering* & false pretences	Acquitted
Auckland SC	23.10.34	Receiving stolen property	1 year & 8 months
Auckland MC	17.12.36	Trespass on racecourse	Fined £2
Auckland SC	2.2.37	Theft	3 months
	8.2.37	Theft	3 months
Auckland MC	16.10.37	Found in common gaming house	Fined £2
Auckland SC	14.2.38	Breaking, entering & theft	9 months
Auckland MC	17.2.38	Theft	Convicted & discharged
		Theft	6 months, cumulative with current sentence
Auckland SC	1.6.39	Breaking, entering & theft (2 charges)	3 years on each
		Receiving	9 months cumulative

Released 28.3.42

*uttering = putting forged money into circulation

about them: the *DNZB* tells us that his first offence was for fraudulently obtaining £14 from two men for posing as a boxer. He was sentenced to probation for this deception, but failed to comply with the terms and ended up in borstal for two years. In 1939 he was sentenced in the Supreme Court to 3 years 9 months on charges of breaking and entering and theft at Te Puke and Tuakau. It was that sentence that ended on 28 March 1942.

But how did this under-educated petty criminal manage to mount and sustain, as we will soon discover, a splendidly successful dramatic performance for five months, from April to August 1942? How did it happen that he aspired to assemble, and bend to his will, such an assorted cast . . . that included army officers, policemen, Cabinet Ministers, and the Prime Minister himself – most of them figures of experience and authority who would be a challenge to any hoodwinker.

To get an answer we must go further back . . . to the Rosses who came to New Zealand from Belfast in the 1840s. George Ross was a soldier – a fencible – who settled in Otahuhu where he and his wife were said to have raised their family in a raupo hut. One supposes they were a lively couple, as their children proved to be unusually articulate, and over the years they, in turn, produced children who were great talkers – good at squeezing entertaining anecdotes out of mundane events. They stood out in a rather dour and taciturn community; generally the Rosses and their descendants were 'fun to be with'.

George Ross had a grandson called Charles (born 1877) who had nine very articulate children, four boys and five girls. Syd was their fourth child.

A family story records the hiring of a local hall and the staging of variety shows – varied performances that would include 'sketches' (very short plays that quickly built to unlikely funny punchlines) – an embryo, perhaps, of the great hoax that one of their number would mount years later. No doubt the home was full of lively rehearsals and discussions.

As they grew up the boys and girls diverged. The sisters became women with strong characters who respected and supported conventional views of right and wrong, while the brothers grew mischievous and troublesome. We can guess a simple psychology at work, as one lot sparked off the other. No doubt the girls grew outraged at the teasing capers and inventions of their brothers, while the boys were challenged to even more audacity by the censure and disapproval of their sisters.

Of the four boys, Syd was *special*. His nephew remembered him as a memorable companion 'full of magic', with a charming want of respect for authority, and conversations that took unexpected twists and turns. He had a knack of presenting a ludicrous idea, and at once shoring it up with colour and invented detail that rendered it credible . . . well, just credible.

Later companions of his in Waikeria prison – where he was head cook – tell of his remarkable skills as a storyteller. They recall sitting about after busy workdays in the kitchen while Syd took them on flights of fancy. Over months he convinced his prison workmates that he was personally known to Adolf Hitler – in fact in close touch with him from day to day; and that the German dictator was sympathetic to the unfair fate of this high-spirited New Zealander locked in a dreary prison deep in the interior of a distant South Pacific island. Indeed, they learned that Hitler would not forget his friendship with Ross when the war was over, and that the Führer and his hierarchy would see to it that he and his circle of mates would be well looked after.

As it happens, the third cook at Waikeria was later to tell – in a statement to the police – of Ross's deadpan tales of friendship with Adolf Hitler, which was so close that the busy dictator found time to write notes to his distant friend, and even indulgently pop some money in the envelope for those little treats that mean so much to a man who is locked up:

> ... Ross told me something about being in Hitler's pay ... we were there in the cookhouse together and he said something about letting him in on 200 pounds and there would be more later on. He just gave me to understand that he was getting money from Hitler ... he was getting sealed letters into the prison from Hitler or his agents. He didn't actually say what the letters contained but he gave me to understand there was money in them. He told me that if Hitler came to power in this country, he (Ross) would be one of the Heads, and he would get me a job as one of his secretaries ... On another occasion Ross told me that when Hitler came to power he would get all the officers (of the prison) and mow them down. He would have them all lined up and shot ...

It would be hard to think of a more implausible tale to test the skills of a storyteller in 1942. If only he had stayed on the right side of the law Syd Ross might now be a celebrated master of comic invention: an actor or a film-maker ... or a novelist, perhaps.

Acquaintances tell of Ross's wide, innocent eyes that held you while he told a story, and validated the truth of it ... and a tremble at the corner of his mouth that suggested private thoughts that played somewhere behind the visible mask, giving hints of an unsuspected world beyond. Another acquaintance told me that he seemed 'constantly on the brink of saying something ... that never got said'.

His brothers were not so special. While Syd was puckish and full of fun but never violent and ill-tempered, his brother Charlie (born in 1900) was generally known as a bad egg – a rougher, tougher type who was often in serious trouble with the law. Described in the *Police Gazette* as a 'blacksmith and entertainer' with twenty convictions, he died violently, beheaded in a sawmill accident.

Two younger brothers also had brushes with the law, and one was rumoured to have more than one 'wife'.

The descendants of George Ross, the fencible of Otahuhu, are now spread around New Zealand, though chiefly in Auckland. Those who have kept in touch agree that family traits that remind them of Syd are still alive – an engaging sense of humour, an interest in dramatic situations, and quick-wittedness, with a beguiling charm. It turned out to be a great mix for an aspiring master-hoaxer.

CHAPTER 2

THE HOAX GETS
UNDER WAY

The train pulled into the big, fairly new Wellington railway station early on the morning of Sunday 29 March 1942. Possibly Ross found the splendid mirrored dining hall and enjoyed a mixed grill for breakfast.

He then checked into the Hotel Waterloo, which was then a spanking new super-modern creation, with a stylish art deco, fully tiled bathroom for every suite, and a coloured telephone on a low coffee table with smart chairs to match . . . a glimpse of the world to come that New Zealanders saw only in the latest films from Hollywood (the Waterloo is still there, of course, right over the road from the station, though now reduced to a backpackers' hostel). By choosing this smart hotel Syd Ross kept faith with himself, seeing to it that his future would be as near to make-believe as he could make it, and absolutely different from that dreary prison existence he had so recently left. In his well-appointed quarters he took a bath to relax himself and get rid of the smuts and grey stains that were the penalties of travelling on a long distance train drawn by a coal-burning locomotive.

By mid-morning, breakfasted, bathed and decked in a fresh shirt, Ross started to put his great design into action by making a call, on his new coloured telephone. For this first contact he had chosen a well-known public figure who prided himself on being a practical man of action . . . not a cerebral reflective man who might question and doubt, but a rough and ready fellow who could be flattered and won over by a simple tale that had a strong thread of logic and drama running through it.

The man whose Sunday morning was to be disturbed was the Honourable Bob Semple, Minister of Public Works (and presently Minister for National Service). Semple was a boisterous extrovert who came originally from Australia, and was partial to issues presented in graphic stories. He was a lively public speaker with a fund of down-to-earth phrases – *'As a government we're off and away with our running shoes on . . .'* – and a habit of livening up a ministerial visit to a public works project by picking up a shovel and working away with it with everyone else – as a labourer uncorrupted by high political office who was not fussed at getting his hands and boots dirty. He was a character.

Now he was held by a telephone informant with an astonishing tale to tell. The man told him that he had arrived in Wellington that very morning . . . a jailbird who had just been released from Waikeria prison . . . and that when he reached Te Awamutu railway station he had been sought out by a well-dressed stranger, who drew him aside and introduced himself as Mr Barnett. After pleasantries this man swore him to secrecy, and then in a low voice told him that he had traced him to that station platform on behalf of a group of right-thinking New Zealanders who had teamed up with a handful of valiant Germans who had landed from a long-range U-boat, with plans to bring the war to New Zealand by blowing up dams, power cables and bridges in the centre of the North Island . . . for which tasks they could do with the skills of an experienced safe-blower like Ross himself. Further, Semple learned that, in the mayhem that would follow these explosions, the German invaders planned to travel to Wellington to hunt down and assassinate senior members of government, including the now-very-interested Minister of Public Works. The well-dressed Mr Barnett was, Semple learned, sure that Ross would join these plotters because he knew he would be bitter and resentful against the leaders of a government that had kept him locked up in wretched and demeaning confinement in a harsh corner of the country for the last three years.

Syd Ross finished his tale by reporting that Barnett then said that he would be in touch again soon . . . and that talk then drifted on to other matters, like the wealth and power that would be his reward when the armed forces of the triumphant fascist Axis powers installed new leaders in New Zealand to replace the present bunch of populist incompetents.

Ross's tale ended with Barnett departing abruptly, leaving him to ponder the rich prospects he had been offered . . . but for which, Semple was assured, he could raise little enthusiasm . . . he was a loyal Kiwi who had no taste for sabotage and assassination, so had promptly made up his mind to hurry to Wellington to raise the alarm . . . and here he was spilling the beans to a senior Cabinet Minister.

What Ross did not know was that the fable he had just passed to the minister had scored a bull's eye – because it fitted a raft of confidential stories that had flowed by cable over the past week from Australia, and reached Semple, as a Cabinet Minister. Semple had learned that, over the Tasman, a disaffected group who called themselves Australia First had formed a spy ring of twenty or so traitors who planned to help any Japanese forces that invaded Australia. The New Zealand Cabinet had been informed that the Australian Minister for the Army, Mr Forde, had seen documents seized by the army that proved the truth of the story, and that he was about to break the news to the press, saying that all twenty traitors had been arrested and charged with treasonable conspiracy.

So what was Semple to make of this roughly similar tale of treason and conspiracy, telephoned from this most unlikely member of the New Zealand public? After all, Semple must have thought, his informant could not possibly have known about the worrying events in

Australia, and it was not too surprising that rat-bags like Australia First would have a few cobbers on this side of the Tasman. Indeed, it would be surprising if those Australia First conspirators over the Tasman had no similarly disaffected oddballs over here . . . wouldn't it?

'Why don't you go to the police with your story?' was Semple's obvious first question.

'Why?' countered Ross. 'Because they wouldn't believe me for a second . . . they know me too well . . . they'd think that I was lying. Who's going to believe a fellow who's spent the last few years in jail? No, they'd probably charge me with wasting police time and pull me out of circulation, and the Germans and their friends would be free to get on with their plans . . .'.

It all hung together . . . for Bob Semple the risk that this Ross fellow and his alarming story was right on to something was just too great to brush off.

Semple said he would think things over and ring back – but he did a little more than that. He rang the Prime Minister, the Right Honourable Peter Fraser, at his office on the third floor of Parliament, just five minutes walk from the Hotel Waterloo. He was hard at work as usual. Bob Semple asked – could he bring round a fellow who had just rung him with a pretty amazing story that just might have some truth in it? – something along the lines of that Forde business in Australia about traitors and saboteurs . . . yes, that arrest of traitors stuff that was to be made public tomorrow . . .

The Prime Minister heard the words *traitor, sabotage, conspiracy* and was interested, and agreed to see Semple and his informant in his office, after lunch. Semple rang Ross back at the Hotel Waterloo and arranged to meet him on the steps of Parliament just before the appointed time.

How would Ross's story and ability as an actor stand up to the test of capturing the subtle and cautious mind of the Prime Minister . . . ?

CHAPTER 3

THE PRIME MINISTER IS DRAWN IN

Semple and Ross called on the Prime Minister in his office in Parliament during the early afternoon of Sunday 29 March 1942. Peter Fraser was an austere figure, stooped and balding, with strong glasses set in small steel frames before half-closed eyes. He was widely respected, rather than loved, for his political ability and determination to lead New Zealand through World War II to a rational and humane world beyond. His successful career was astonishing for a man who spoke freely on platforms or over the radio, but sounded so un-New Zealand . . . especially, there was that un-Kiwi voice, straight from the north of the British Isles with its unfamiliar tone, emphases and pronunciations – Scottish without the burr or rolling r's that we expect from Scots, delivered with a way that was often mimicked and tagged parsonical. From him motor cars became 'mutter cars', New Zealand was 'Noo Zillin' and a million pounds were 'a million-puns'.

Fraser's political career had spanned most of the first half of the twentieth century. He was deputy prime minister in 1935 under the Labour Prime Minister Michael Joseph Savage, and had proved an outstanding Minister of Education. He became prime minister in 1940, and was already a considerable world figure.

No doubt the Prime Minister had well in mind the breaking story about the Australia First spy ring that was even then being released to the New Zealand press. It was to be the lead news story in Wellington's *Evening Post* the next day, under the heading 'Alleged Spy Ring – Dramatic Story – Australian Sensation'. Fraser knew all too well the precarious position New Zealand was in, as a small, almost defenceless, sparsely-populated island nation in the South Pacific, closely menaced by Japanese armed forces that had sunk much of the US fleet at Pearl Harbor, and now, only four months later, had reached Australia and New Guinea.

From the perspective of the twenty-first century it is easy to look back on World War II as a cataclysmic conflict – perhaps the most dramatic series of events in human history – that was in the end inevitably won by the might of the Allied forces of fairness and justice over the sinister Axis forces of evil and aggression. But in the early months of 1942 that outcome was not inevitable at all, and the tide looked to be running in favour of the Axis powers. There seemed to be a strong chance that Germany, Japan and Italy would be successful, and that Britain, America, Russia and their allies would lose the war.

I, the author of this book, and aged thirteen in 1942, can remember the horror and despair that ordinary New Zealanders felt at the numbing and dispiriting series of defeats and reverses that were reported daily in the newspapers and regular news bulletins broadcast from London by the BBC. The loss of France and the escape at Dunkirk, the blitz on London, the success of Hitler's armies in Russia (they came within sight of Moscow), the reverses in North Africa, and the violent attack on Pearl Harbor in December 1941 with the destruction of most of the US Pacific fleet, and then the swift Japanese advance down through Malaya, Singapore and the Dutch East Indies to Australia itself. It seemed impossible that the Allies could gather the strength to turn this powerful tide. What would happen to us?

Families that followed these awful events closely, as mine did, felt that a cataclysm was on the way. It was as though we had news that a huge asteroid was headed towards Earth from deep space and timed to strike in a month or two . . . and what would happen after that? I remember waking in the small hours of the morning wondering just that . . . when the Japanese came, would we survive? If we did, what would the world be like? (We could not know, of course, that the first half of 1942 was the lowest point of the war, and that in a few months the tide was to turn with the naval battle of Midway in the Pacific and huge Russian successes at Stalingrad and Kursk, and the advances of the Eighth Army in North Africa.)

Peter Fraser was fully engaged in the struggle at the crucial time before the turning point of World War II. As New Zealand seemed in the path of Japanese aggressive advance, while our young men were thousands of miles away in North Africa battling Rommel's Afrika Korps, Fraser broadcast to the nation (8 March 1942): '. . . let there be no doubt . . . if there is a raid we will repulse it . . . if there is an invasion we will hurl it back. But we must work as never before to do this. Anybody who shirks or obstructs in any way is an enemy who cannot be excused.'

Newspapers for the weekend on which Ross reached Wellington reported alarming news – for example, Dr Evatt, the Australian Minister of External Affairs, announced that without doubt the Japanese would '. . . attack both Australia and India, and do so at once . . . experts were deliberating on whether Japan would attack India or Australia . . . It seems plain enough that Japan would attack both.'

Indeed, the very next day Wellington's *Evening Post* (2.4.42) reported that Darwin had been hit by waves of Japanese bombers for the seventh time, and Port Moresby, in New Guinea, for the twenty-first time; and the same paper reported that the Japanese were grouping half a million men in Manchuria to attack Russia. The whole Pacific was alight with advancing menace.

In the same issue of the *Post* a news item, printed in bold, told that a Pacific War Council had been formed, and that Mr Fraser was pleased. On the same page we read about a lively gathering in Hamilton – 'Awake New Zealand' – to meet the Prime Minister.

When Syd Ross and Bob Semple were admitted to the Prime Minister's office it is likely that he had on his desk the worrying report of the Australian Minister for the Army, Mr Forde, that was soon to appear in the capital's morning paper the *Dominion*, telling of 'plans for the assassination of prominent people and plans for sabotage at vulnerable points in Australia, and detailed methods calculated to make resistance to the Japanese [invaders] impossible'. Another seized document planned to 'welcome to this country as friends and liberators the Japanese leaders and army'.

And now into his office was ushered a man, who, Mr Fraser was to discover, had a tale of a remarkably similar group in New Zealand. Ross's story of being approached by a mysterious Mr Barnett would have been repeated, no doubt with more circumstantial details, and with more assurance than the first telling earlier in the day that had impressed Bob Semple. Ross, unaware of the news from Australia, must have been gratified by the close attention of his audience.

Of course, verifiable truth and utter falsehood were mixed in Syd Ross's tale. *True*, he had just been released from prison; *true*, he had travelled from Te Awamutu overnight; *true,* the police would not believe a word of his story; *false* was the appearance of Mr Barnett and his alarming news and tempting offer. Ross blended a tale that had enough truth in it to convince his audience, especially as it fitted so closely Mr Forde's breaking news from Australia.

No doubt Fraser probed and tested the story, but in the end he decided that it was credible . . . after all, why shouldn't a petty criminal be opposed to sabotage and assassination? As Ross insisted, for seemingly good reasons, that the matter could not be handed over to the police, the Prime Minister decided to call in the recently formed army unit that specialised in security matters: the Security Intelligence Bureau, whose head, Major Kenneth Folkes, was at that moment relaxing after Sunday dinner at his home in Wellington's northern suburb of Wadestown.

A phone call summoned Folkes to the Prime Minister's office to discuss an urgent matter of national security: he slipped on his uniform and drove at once to Parliament Buildings.

In Mr Fraser's office he found Mr Semple and a tall stranger with thin brown hair and a long nose. Without delay they settled down and heard Ross's story told for the third time, no doubt recounted even more convincingly than before, with a peppering of credible, newly invented details that put the truth of it beyond doubt.

At the end of the telling there would have been some discussion, in which Ross would have no doubt been fascinated to find that his story was being validated by some facts that were known to his three listeners – something about Australia – but about which he knew nothing.

Folkes was ordered to look into the matter, and he and Ross were dismissed from the Prime Ministerial presence. They arranged to meet the following morning (Monday) and Ross returned to his hotel; Folkes rejoined his family in Wadestown.

The next day Syd Ross and Major Folkes met, probably in the SIB offices on the corner of Featherston and Hunter

Streets. They would have gone over the previous day's discussions with the Prime Minister, and then quickly decided that Ross would be given an alias (Captain Calder of the Merchant Marine was decided on) and a cover story – that he was on leave in New Zealand while his ship was under repair. He would be given a car so that he could travel easily, and all the vouchers and passes he would need to secure petrol (strictly rationed in 1942) and hotel accommodation. Because the supposed plotters he was to keep an eye on were thought to be near Rotorua, Ross (now 'Calder') would be passed to the Auckland office of the SIB under Captain Meikle, whose control extended to the central North Island.

The following evening Captain Calder, decked out in the uniform of a captain in the Merchant Navy, left for Auckland. He went by train, but this time in a comfortable sleeping compartment, as fitted his new rank.

In Wellington, Folkes used his secure telephone line to let Meikle in Auckland know what was afoot, and then took some days to consider how to act on the matter that had been dropped in his lap. How could Ross's story possibly be false? What reason could this jailbird have for telling lies – and lies that in the fullness of time would be found out and get him into deep trouble? Ross was, after all, not asking for money! To see through Ross and even glimpse the deep well of acting ability and inventiveness that lay hidden there, Folkes would have needed a sense of humour, and the wit to probe the mind of someone who thought very differently from himself. That was not part of the Major's make-up.

And if the tale were true there was the prospect of a heroic future for the SIB and enormous elevation for its principal officer.

On Saturday 4 April Folkes wrote a brief, rather astonishing, note to the Prime Minister:

The Rt. Hon. The Prime Minister
New Zealand

Sir,

With regard to the interview I had with you on Sunday afternoon last, investigations prove that the story we heard has substance. The matter is developing slowly and is leading to a clique already under notice.

Further developments will be reported to you immediately.

I have the honour to be, sir,
Your obedient servant
signed K. Folkes   Major G.S.

So, Captain Calder's oft-repeated tale had gained a lot of weight, for already the Director of Security was writing a letter to the Prime Minister telling him that it 'has substance', and that the nest of German conspirators that Ross invented are real and organised in a clique that he, Folkes, already knows of!

Over the weeks that followed Folkes went on to write a series of letters to the Prime Minister, increasing in urgency and concern and supported by lists of names and other details based on news sent to him by Ross, whom we must now call Calder. None of these notes has come to light excepting one dated 10 June 1942, in which the number of reported conspirators has swelled to twenty, and matters seem to be coming to a head.

I will reproduce this June letter here in full because it shows a change in the scale of the whole affair. An elaborate prank, planned to relieve the boredom of an imaginative criminal (Ross), has been catapulted into a national emergency, with a predicted enemy invasion within a month:

P.O. Box 775,
WELLINGTON.

10th June, 1942

Sir,

I have the honour to record, as directed
by you, the facts, as I known them, concerning an organisation
operating in this Dominion, for the purpose of fifth column
activities in assisting an invading force in the conquest of
this country.

Simply, but plainly, the position is as follows:
There is established in the centre of the North Island a
Headquarters of this organisation, at the head of which is
an elderly man with a criminal record in this country, and
I believe , in England.   I am satisfied that the name by
which he has been known in this country for many years is
not his true name.   Closely associated with him are several
persons of foreign origin or association. The existence of
some of these persons is unknown to the Authorities, and I am
satisfied that they entered this country by unlawful means.
Also connected with this organisation in a lesser degree are
two New Zealanders, one a journalist and the other an expert
wireless technician at present holding a post in the most
important Wireless Station in the North Island. The total
number of persons involved - so far as can be at present
ascertained - is as follows:

          14 Germans
           1 Russian
           1 Hungarian
           1 Asiatic (believed Japanese)
           1 Swiss
           2 New Zealanders

After many weeks observation and surveillance, the
following plan emerges: Immediately prior to the invasion
(which is confidently predicted within the organisation)
counterfeit money is to be circulated, rumours disseminated,
water-works, tunnels and viaducts to be destroyed.   The
assassination of important Ministers is freely discussed
between the parties as the culminating factor in the
destruction of public morale as a basis for successful invasion.

To implement this plan, the organisation obviously
requires persons experienced in the use of explosives and
gunmen.   They have already enlisted the aid of an expert

in the use of gelignite - who has been detailed to perform the
destruction of ARAPUNI and WAIKAREMOANA WATERWORKS. The
explosives required are available at any time. This expert
is now about to enlist the aid of other persons up and down
the country whose functions will be localised in their own
particular district. The organisation has already enlisted
a marksman. In this connection it is important to observe
that four of its members are armed, night and day. Highly
subversive pamphlets are already in draft form. Soon after
I commenced investigations into this case, I was able to sheet
home to a soldier at Trentham the authorship of a pamphlet
(copy of which is attached). It so happened that I was able
to prevent distribution of this pamphlet without impairing
investigations into the organisation as a whole. The case of
the soldier in question - one KLEIN - who is linked with the
organisation - is now engaging the attention of the Solicitor-
General.

At this stage it is convenient to discuss:

(a) When the plan is to be put into effect
(b) What steps are to be taken by the Government
to prevent it

With regard to (a) I opine that it is likely to
occur sometime in July. It is clear that the leader of the
organisation in this country is expecting intelligence to
reach him by the arrival of one, probably two, individuals
from outside the Dominion. The event has been delayed it
seems, but pending that, plans are being carefully formulated.
I suspect that these individuals will come from Australia, but
I may be wrong. Certainly, the wireless technician referred
to was recently detailed to visit Australia - via the Tasman
Air Service, and all arrangements were made for him to do so
but through events, over which he had no control, he was
prevented from travelling. Again, while I have no tangible
evidence of the New Zealand organisation being linked with the
one recently uncovered in Australia, there is a significant
similarity in aims. For your information I send you a summary
of intelligence concerning The First Australia Movement, which
as you know, is the subject of a criminal trial at present being
held in Australia.

With regard to (b), I have to make it perfectly plain
that I am unable to adduce evidence which would fix the guilt
of the parties concerned within the ordinary criminal code.
The reason for this is the acute appreciation of the organisation
of the desirability of avoiding details of their plans being
reduced into writing and for clandestine meetings and secret
conversations. Therefore, to bring them within the criminal
code it would be necessary to produce indisputable viva voce
testimony concerning the conspiracy. This is impossible to

do at this stage. But I wish to make it equally plain
that if the Government takes unto itself the powers hereunder
referred to I believe that as a result of the exercise of those
powers, I will be able -

      (a)   to prevent the plan being carried into effect
      (b)   prove the conspiracy.

     Every possible action has been taken by me to prove
the truth or otherwise of intelligence which I have received,
by checking and cross-checking, and in every single case where
this has been possible, the result has been positive. In other
words, I believe my Informant. The question arises, therefore, what is to be done? As I have said above, I cannot make
out a case for a criminal trial. Except for a sheer fluke
(upon which I cannot rely) it is extremely unlikely that I
would be able to make out a case, until after the plan had
been put into effect. To allow the latter course is un-
thinkable and, therefore, one is forced to the view that the
Government must take the powers contained in 18(b) of the
Defence Act in the United Kingdom. If these powers be taken
then they would be invoked at a time to be decided - according
to the trend of events, In this connection, I would stress
two points. The first is that I cannot guarantee when action
would be necessary. (It could quite conceivably be required
within a week). The second point is that a considerable
number of persons would be required to act in various places
in the Dominion, all at the same time, and for arrangements
to be made for those persons apprehended (likely to be
approximately one hundred) to be held incommunicado
These arrangements would necessarily be extremely intricate
and detailed .

     If, on the other hand, it is decided not to take the
powers, then may I respectfully say that while the most
strenuous endeavours will be made to prevent the plan being
carried into effect, I could not undertake complete responsibility
in that connection. I am constrained to say this because
I am satisfied that we are dealing with desperate men, and
particularly so, in the case of the individual directing
operations.

           I have the honour to be,

               Sir,

The Rt.Hon.P.Fraser,P.C.   Your obedient servant,
Prime Minister of New Zealand
WELLINGTON.   MAJOR. G.S.
           DIRECTOR. SECURITY INTELLIGENCE

What an astonishing and reckless letter! In it New Zealand's Director of Security hijacks Captain Calder's cheeky molehill of a personal hoax and re-invents it as a mountainous urgent threat to the security of New Zealand, and the personal safety of the Prime Minister himself. Folkes was a senior army officer (with a salary equal to that of the Chief of Staff), so that his letter to Peter Fraser validating Calder's tale, and then inflating it wildly, must signal that there is more here than meets the eye, and that Folkes has devised an agenda of his own, and is now following it.

Major Folkes's letter that reported to the Prime Minister the existence of a sinister twenty-man organisation which was planning all sorts of mischief was, of course, a tissue of perils that he had invented . . . but the Major's second contention, that to meet this supposed danger '. . . government must take the powers contained in 18(b) of the Defence Act of the United Kingdom', had a connection with reality, as 18(b) was indeed a real regulation in force in the UK Sections 18(a), 18(b) and 18(c) (and many more) had been added to the original Defence (General) Regulations of 25 August 1939 by amendment 927 on 23 November 1939. Under this legislation, administered by the British Home Office, men and women of doubtful loyalty, including members of Sir Oswald Mosley's British Union of Fascists, and no doubt other Fascist sympathisers, were imprisoned in the early years of World War II. When the danger of German invasion passed the regulations were revoked in September 1944.

To make sense of the sudden explosive inflation of the story I think it will be best to interrupt the narrative of Captain Calder's comfortable progress in a sleeping compartment of the Express train to Auckland and the adventures that followed, and find out instead about Major Kenneth Folkes, Director of Security and Head of the SIB . . . and why he has decided to take Calder's cock-and-bull story and make it his own. We will then be able to make something of the scraps of 'evidence' in the letter – particularly the radio technician '. . . at present holding a post at the most important wireless station in the North Island . . .' and the journalist, and the '. . . elderly man with a criminal record in this country under a false name . . .'

CHAPTER 4

THE SECURITY
INTELLIGENCE BUREAU

When World War II broke out, British military chiefs found that Britain's Commonwealth no longer comprised the awed subservient states that had followed Britain in 1914. Several of the Dominions were now independent nations – countries that would make up their own minds, and act according to due processes of law and decision-making on questions that were of great moment to them. Particularly, the small group of intensely loyal South Pacific islands called New Zealand could volunteer good support only when their government was closely and continuously informed of what was going on on the Allied side.

If a flow of confidential information was to reach New Zealand, then a service must be set up there to make sure that the secrets were properly guarded and managed – a service equivalent, in miniature, to Britain's security intelligence services MI5 and MI6.

A security intelligence service was duly established and led by Lieut. Colonel J.C. Mawhood. Some training was shared, in Australia, with Australian forces, but it was then decided that the New Zealand bureau must be kept in close touch with the source of most of the secrets – Britain – by appointing a director from within the United Kingdom security establishment. Accordingly, a service called the New Zealand Security Intelligence Bureau was set up, and an officer sent from Britain to lead it and keep close links with British security services. This man was Lieutenant Kenneth Folkes, who was promoted and arrived in New Zealand as Major Folkes.

Folkes replaced Mawhood, but from the beginning he proved to be out of sympathy with the armed services of his new country – from his first day here he was shocked by the easy-going ways of New Zealanders. They seemed to him to be much too sloppy and informal, and he set about showing an example to his Bureau, and to anyone else he met in the armed services, by his own smartness and brusque formality. He detested a newspaper cartoon character of the war years called 'Old Soldier Sam', who was a rather scruffy figure of fun in a lemon-squeezer hat, baggy army trousers and shapeless service jacket who seemed to the Major to encapsulate what was regrettable about too many of the New Zealand servicemen and servicewomen he came across.

A common story has it that when Folkes first reported to the Prime Minister he contrived to have his appointment at half past ten – just at morning tea time – and slipped into the empty administrative office and typing area to move quietly among the vacated desks, lifting a selection of assorted papers – one from here and one from there from 'in' and 'out' trays – and flicking them into his brief-case. Two minutes later he was able to produce these prizes to the startled Prime Minister . . . 'Look, Sir, at your lax security arrangements . . . here in the last few minutes I have already gathered this collection of confidential papers . . . anyone could have taken them . . . your office is unguarded and vulnerable . . .'

Naturally the secretaries and typists were furious. What Fraser thought is not recorded.

When Major Kenneth Folkes settled to his task he came to see that the job of his Security Intelligence Bureau had three parts to it. The first was to find, and deal with, any New Zealanders of dubious loyalty who might somehow subvert the war effort or even spy for the enemy Axis powers. The second task was to guard the coasts around

New Zealand against penetration, and deal in a routine way with innocent breaches of our frontiers by travellers such as local fishermen, or visitors on passenger ships. Finally, the Bureau had to watch carefully the stream of confidential papers from overseas that New Zealand was then privy to – to devise and carry out routines and systems to limit who could be allowed to see them, and how they were to be discreetly handled and securely stored . . . and expressly how these precious papers were to be secured when they were sent on from New Zealand in allied ships that were always in danger of being captured and searched by enemy warships or raiders.

The first of these tasks proved easy enough because it turned out that New Zealanders were a remarkably loyal and undivided people in the face of potential enemy attack and invasion. In fact, there was no significant pro-Axis group or faction, nor any German or Japanese spies to hunt down. There was no New Zealand equivalent of Australia's Australia First movement that surfaced so spectacularly in early 1942. There was, sometimes, loose talk on trams or in bars (and occasionally the chatterers were tracked down and talked to sternly), but never any real fear that information might reach German or Japanese spies, because there were none.

A few Axis supporters were marooned in New Zealand when war broke out, and these unfortunates were easily found and imprisoned or banished to Somes Island in Wellington Harbour. In fact, rather too many were rounded up, for New Zealanders were not good at distinguishing one ideology from another, so that some who had escaped here from Nazi Germany suffered the indignity of being locked up with real Nazi internees or prisoners for company.

It was astonishing that German wartime propaganda broadcasts to New Zealand apparently scored absolutely no successes here. In the years before World War II the widely-read weekly the *New Zealand Radio Record*, published in Wellington and soon to be incorporated in the *New Zealand Listener*, included a regular half-page display headed 'Germany Calling' that set out the short-wave programmes from Berlin that were to be broadcast the following week, including news and commentaries and regular concerts by artists such as the Hitler Youth Choir. These politically loaded English-language broadcasts could be picked up very clearly by any New Zealander whose radio was wired for short-wave . . . as most new radios were in those days.

From the mid-1930s domestic radio sets were assembled in New Zealand and proved remarkably efficient at receiving foreign radio broadcasts. Most had a control knob that switched to receive short wave, and the big glass-covered dials (usually back-lit by several small light bulbs) were often elaborately printed to locate foreign radio stations – promising sources such as **Paris, Moscow, Berlin, London,** or **Madrid.** Radio reception, particularly in the evenings, was often very clear indeed.

During the war Berlin broadcast regular two hourly late afternoon short-wave programmes in its Pacific Service for New Zealand listeners (I know, because I – then a schoolboy – used to listen to them, fascinated to hear voices coming directly from Berlin – the centre of the enemy empire! How chilling to hear a curt 'Heil Hitler' at the end of a news broadcast, read in flawless, but ever-so-slightly-Germanic English! – though I have never heard of any other New Zealander who listened even once to Radio Berlin). At all events it seems that all that broadcasting effort, day after day and year after year, scored no successes for the busy Nazi propagandists.

The second matter (frontier protection) was dealt with routinely and competently enough, with armed security officers sent to sea with New Zealand's ocean fishing boats (though whether the Italian fishermen were being

Germany Calling N.Z.

Below are details of the special shortwave programmes to be broadcast for listeners in Australia, New Zealand and Southern Asia from Germany next week. New Zealand summer time is given.

The programmes on this page may be heard from the following short-wave stations :—

DJB . . . 19.74m.
DJN . . . 31.45m.

SUNDAY, DECEMBER 15.
8.45 p.m.: Call DJB, DJN (German, English). German folk song. Programme forecast (Germ., Engl.).
9.0: Hitler Youth programme: "Poets in the Hitler Youth." Herbert Boehme."
9.15: Sonata in C Major, Op. 102 for 'Cello and Piano, by Ludwig van Beethoven.
9.30: News and review of the week in English.
9.45: Brahms hour: Dirge for Contralto Choir and Orchestra; Symphony No. 4 in C Minor. Margarete Arndt-Ober, the German Choral Union. Conductor: W. Richter-Reichhelm.
11.0: Concert of light music.
12.0: News and review of the week in English.

MONDAY, DECEMBER 16.
8.45 p.m.: Call DJB, DJN (German, English). German folk song. Programme forecast (Germ., Engl.).
9.0: Relayed from Berlin: "Christmas Shopping." A visit to the Berlin Christmas Fair.
9.30: News in English.

9.45: Folk songs.
9.50: Technical letter box.
10.0: "I Should Like . . ." Verse, songs and music.
11.0: Concert of light music.
12.0: News in English.

TUESDAY, DECEMBER 17.
8.45 p.m.: Call DJB, DJN (German, English). German folk song. Programme forecast (Germ., Engl.).
9.0: Hitler Youth programme: Folk song singing by the Hitler Youth.
9.15: From manuscripts of Dutch composers of the 18th century.
9.30: News in English.
9.45: Christmas poems. Kate Gold.
10.0: Old German festival tunes and dances.
11.0: Concert of light music.
12.0: News in English.

WEDNESDAY, DEC. 18.
8.45 p.m.: Call DJB, DJN (German, English). German folk song. Programme

forecast (Germ., Engl.). Letter box.
9.0: Sonata for 'Cello and Piano, by Hans Pfitzner. Ludwig Hoelscher and the composer.
9.30: News in English.
9.45: "Christmas with Germans in the Borderlands and Overseas." Compiled and arranged by Heinrich Werle.
10.45: News in German.
11.0: Concert of light music.
12.0: News in English.

THURSDAY, DECEMBER 19
8.45 p.m.: Call DJB, DJN (German, English). German folk song. Programme forecast (Germ., Engl.).
9.0: Hitler Youth programme: "The Nation's Youth."
9.30: News in English.
9.45: Philharmonic concert. Conductor: Wilhelm Furtwaengler. Soloist: Georg Kulenkampff.
10.45: News in German.
11.0: Concert of light music.

11.20: Topical talk.
11.30: Concert of light music (continued).
12.0: News in English.

FRIDAY, DECEMBER 20.
8.45 p.m.: Call DJB, DJN (German, English). German folk song. Programme forecast (Germ., Engl.).
9.0: "German Masters of Song." Songs by Brahms and Wolf, sung by Tiana Lemnitz.
9.30: News in English.
9.45: Brass band.
10.45: News in German.
12.0: News in English.

SATURDAY, DECEMBER 21.
8.45 p.m.: Call DJB, DJN (German, English). German folk song. Programme forecast (Germ., Engl.).
9.0: Woman's hour: "The King and the Maiden Tall." A musical comedy by Hans Feineis.
9.30: News in English.
9.45: Quintet for Guitar and String Quartet, by Boccherini and Schnabel. Hans Neemann and the Sedding Quartet.
10.30: Jocular songs and song jokes.
10.45: News in German.
11.0: Concert of light music.
12.0: News in English.

Nazi Propaganda. This information about nightly radio programmes that were broadcast from Germany by shortwave transmissions originated with one of the German secret services. Similar programme summaries were published each week in the *New Zealand Radio Record* (a weekly that became incorporated in the *New Zealand Listener*) until World War II broke out in September 1939.

protected from attack, or watched for possible treacherous contact with enemy ships, is not clear). All wharves were watched over by guards.

The third matter – the guarding of strategically sensitive papers – proved to be a much more worrying matter, where small, seemingly trivial slips occasionally had vast and disastrous consequences.

A lot has been published about the astonishing wartime successes of the Allied code-breakers, and particularly of the British government's code and cipher school that moved to Bletchley Park in 1938, and set about accumulating a team of specialists who began to unpick Germany's radio codes, sent by morse signals, that Hitler and his military commanders believed were absolutely unbreakable, and so of huge strategic use to the Third Reich's planned conquest of Europe and beyond. Indeed, Bletchley's part in breaking these and other German, Italian and Japanese codes is now acknowledged to have been of immense importance to the ultimate Allied victory in 1945 (in 1943 the world's first programmable electronic computer – Colossus – was developed to break high-grade German ciphers – a secret that was made known only in 1975).

At the same time the Americans set up some considerable code-breaking centres, particularly in Hawaii.

It is less well known that the Axis powers also scored some successes in the early years of World War II and read quite a number of Allied secret documents. Some were radio signals that were intercepted and decoded (including details of British plans in North Africa that reached Rommel and made it seem that he possessed almost magical powers of prediction), and some were strategic papers that were carried on ships that were stopped and searched by German vessels. The most striking example of this kind of disaster was the seizure from the Allied freighter *Automedon* by the German raider *Atlantis* (Captain Rogge) of copies of frank British

Cabinet papers that made clear Britain's recognition of its own military weakness in the far East. It has often been said that, in Axis hands, these revealing papers must have encouraged Japanese planners to expect that their Pacific aggressions after Pearl Harbor (4 December 1941), particularly against Hong Kong, Singapore and Malaya, would succeed. (See a paper by James Rushbridger in the May 1985 issue of *Encounter*.)

Closer to home in New Zealand is the sorry story of strategically sensitive mail being carelessly loaded without proper safeguards at a New Zealand port onto the Australian freighter *Nankin* in April 1942 (the very same month in which Major Folkes was working to convince the Prime Minister that there was truth in Ross/Calder's fairy story, and that he – Folkes – knew what was to be done). What happened to the *Nankin*, and the precious papers it carried, is summarised from Rushbridger's paper in a *Newsletter* published by the New Zealand Council for Civil Liberties:

By the 5 May 1942 the *Nankin* had reached and left Fremantle in West Australia, bound for Colombo, and five days out was captured by the German raider *Thor*. Among the *Nankin*'s cargo the Germans found a large quantity of mail. The bulk of it was routine, comprising letters and packets from South Africa, New Zealand and Australia destined for England, but there was also a small amount of very secret mail from the Combined Operations Intelligence Centre (COIC) at Wellington, New Zealand, *en route* for Commander-in-Chief Eastern Fleet (Colombo).

COIC (sometimes known as the Central Intelligence Bureau) was first established in 1940 in an office next door to New Zealand's central war room in Stout Street, Wellington. It was an offshoot of the Prime Minister's group called the 'Organisation for National Security' which began work in 1938 keeping records on Japanese (and other aliens) in New Zealand. COIC co-ordinated the intelligence activities of New Zealand's Army, Navy and Air Force and had close links with the Police and Customs Service; it also worked closely with the British, American and Australian Intelligence Services, from which it received a lot of very sensitive information, much of which dealt with matters far outside the Australasian theatre of operations.

Each week COIC issued a 'most secret' intelligence summary which was distributed on an Officer Only basis to 22 named recipients, including the C in C (Commander in Chief) US Pacific Fleet, Admiral Chester Nimitz. A further warning inside each summary stated that the contents came from *Most Secret Sources*, an expression coined by Churchill to denote that the information was of ULTRA classification and had been obtained from cryptanalysis (that is, from deciphered enemy codes).

Each summary was divided into four parts. The first, dealing with information about the ANZAC theatre of operations, gave details of Allied shipping, naval vessels, convoys, and so forth. The second part concerned external intelligence and appears to have covered any part of the world (it included, for example, weekly tonnages arriving in the United Kingdom – which seems a strange piece of information to send all the way out to New Zealand). Part Three provided information on Japanese forces and general comments about the Japanese economy, while Part Four gave a detailed list of the estimated disposition of Japanese naval vessels in the Indian and Pacific Oceans and their likely future movements. A separate appendix gave the latest details of every Allied vessel in the same area, and their future movements.

Clearly it was disastrous that this information should fall into enemy hands!

Some of the information in these summaries came from normal sources such as air reconnaissance, interrogation of prisoners, and the coast watcher service – which involved agents living behind Japanese lines and radioing reports to the Intelligence Services, and analysis of regular radio traffic passing between ships at sea and their land bases.

But it was equally clear that much of the very detailed knowledge of the whereabouts of enemy ships and their intended movements could only have come from code-breaking; and it seems that COIC was receiving a great deal of information from the US Navy's cryptanalysis organisation in Hawaii.

This was known as the Fleet Radio Unit (FRUPAC), which had a subsidiary headquarters in Belconnen in Australia. These two teams of cryptographers had been intercepting, analysing, and slowly penetrating the most complex Japanese operational cipher, which the US Navy called JN25. It involved an elaborate system of double-encipherment using a number of different tables of figure groups, each of which was regularly changed. Although it was not a machine cipher like *Enigma*, or that used by the Japanese for diplomatic communications, it was still considered impossible to break.

The Americans naturally guarded the secret of their code-breaking successes very carefully; and it is not yet clear whether FRUPAC was aware how much information was being passed to COIC, or to what extent COIC was redistributing it. The late Admiral Layton USN (he died in May 1984) was Nimitz's Fleet Radio Officer in charge of all intelligence matters and in close touch with the code-breakers at FRUPAC, and he has said that there was always great concern within the US Navy that such vital information was being passed to organisations outside their control.

Because of the sensitive nature of the COIC summaries it would have been normal procedure, as laid down by the New Zealand Organisation for National Security, for them to be distributed by hand, using a courier, as with similar material from Bletchley Park. One of the great problems about putting the ULTRA material to use was: how to impart the material without compromising the source. Frequently a cover story would be invented to pretend that it came from a spy.

According to a surviving officer from the *Nankin*, no

such courier mail was handed to Captain Stratford. It seems, therefore, that the COIC summaries had inadvertently been included in the general mail – which, considering the large number of vessels captured by German raiders in the previous two years, was an appalling breach of elementary security (it seems that they were not even put into canvas bags containing lead weights that could be thrown overboard if capture threatened – a common precaution in those days).

It has been possible to establish from two of Admiral Wenneker's telegrams from Japan to Berlin that COIC summaries 12, 13, 14 and 15 (covering the period 21 March to 20 April 1942) were on board the *Nankin* and were captured. These particular reports were of crucial importance. They clearly showed the US Navy's increasing knowledge of the Japanese battle fleet's movements in the weeks leading up to the Battle of Midway (3–5 June), and this could only have come from reading the JN25 fleet-cipher.

As a result of the disclosures from the captured Combined Operations Intelligence Centre summaries the Japanese Navy immediately imposed strict new security arrangements to protect the JN25 fleet cipher, and US code-breakers began the laborious task of reconstructing the new cipher tables. But immediately after Admiral Wenneker's meeting with the Japanese on 29 August 1942 they suffered a sudden signals blackout, so total that it was well into 1943 before the US Navy was able to get useful information again.

This loss of signals intelligence seriously affected the outcome of at least three major naval engagements in the Pacific: the battles of Cape Esperance (11–12 October), Santa Cruz (26th October) and Guadalcanal (13–15 October) – all of which resulted in unexpectedly severe losses for the US Navy.

Had details of the COIC mail from the *Nankin* reached Japan more quickly the tremendous US victory at the Battle of Midway (four Japanese aircraft carriers were sunk in one day!) might have been different. All historians agree that that stunning American success turned the tide of the Pacific war and set the United States on the road to victory in 1945. The decisive victory was helped by the US Navy's ability to read the Japanese Navy's ciphers and thus anticipate their intentions. The later loss of this ability seriously reduced the US Navy's fighting ability for many months at a most crucial point in the war, and caused severe American losses in several subsequent naval battles.

CHAPTER 5

MAJOR FOLKES IS
SPIED ON

The secure loading of these crucially sensitive strategic war papers was a task that should have engaged the full attention of the Director of Security, Major Kenneth Folkes, and it is astonishing to learn that his thoughts were in fact elsewhere, inventing a non-existent group of twenty-or-so enemy aliens at Rotorua, and writing to convince the Prime Minister that he had the peril well in check, but needed wide additional powers to coordinate and direct the armed services so that the Security Intelligence Bureau that he headed could keep a sharp eye on these sinister enemies and counter their plans. No doubt he would have liked to have the Police and other civil authorities under his control too.

If things had gone his way, and UK Regulation 18(b) had been invoked in ways that he wanted, Folkes could have been the most powerful man in the country.

But what of the wartime Bureau that Folkes headed?

One might expect that the Security Intelligence Bureau was so secretive and discreet that few traces would be left on the public record after the war ended. As it happens, that was not so, for there was in New Zealand a small, dedicated, ideologically committed group of citizens who learned of Folkes's appointment. Sensing a threat, they made it their business to keep watch on him and his growing SIB, and raise the alarm in their weekly newspaper.

The whistleblower was the Communist Party of New Zealand, and their weekly journal was the *People's Voice*.

New Zealand communists had endured an awkward political position, with the *People's Voice* banned from publication, while the Hitler/Stalin pact was in force, but came in from the cold when Hitler tore up the pact and invaded Russia with barbaric force in June 1941. Britain and Russia were thrown together as allies against Fascist aggression.

The *People's Voice* was still banned as an illegal publication when it broke the news of Folkes's appointment as officer in charge of the New Zealand Security Intelligence Bureau, in its issue of 5 June 1941, to its small circle of surreptitious readers. The issue was roughly typewritten, and run off on an office duplicator (a Roneo or a Gestetner, as the makes were named in those days).

The Communist Party was, by experience, very suspicious of Western security intelligence organisations. Party members remembered many incidents such as the Zinoviev Letter – which had turned out to be a scandalous invention and plant of Britain's MI6, a fraudulent document that mischievously helped to poison relations between Britain and the Soviet Union. The appearance of an enlarged Security Intelligence Bureau in Wellington, headed by a British officer who retained links with the British intelligence service, deepened these suspicions.

To the Communists, Folkes and his bunch fitted into an obvious slot: they recalled images of the Nazi secret police – the Gestapo – so that Folkes was presented to the readers of the *People's Voice* as the South Pacific shadow of Heinrich Himmler, Hitler's deputy in Nazi Germany. In that role the Party saw Folkes as the direct enemy of every patriotic New Zealander, and a direct ideological foe of the Communist Party.

Readers of the *People's Voice* learned that Folkes should be seen as a sly and sinister individual heading a Bureau of layabouts and shirkers, who spent their time in the safety of New Zealand far from the dangers of the battlefront, pimping on honest, hard-working soldiers who were headed for active service against the Fascist enemies that the British Empire shared with Russia.

To show the scale of the SIB establishment the *People's Voice* carefully reported the staff in each office, with the names of the officers in each, and often some brief notes.

The paragraphs that follow come directly from the *People's Voice* – although a few of the most unkind personal descriptions of SIB members have been trimmed because they may well cause distress to some who are still alive, and may be unfair to those who can no longer respond. The cuts are marked thus . . .

Who is the second best paid soldier in New Zealand? **Major Kenneth Folkes**, £1,100-a-year head of the Dominion's Gestapo, an assortment of mediocre journalists, clerks and even 'counter jumpers'. Folkes himself was gazetted an acting lieutenant in the Imperial Army little more than a year ago (July, 1940). This was not in a fighting force, but in the British security police; in fact what Folkes does not know about soldiering was indicated by a recent appearance at Army Headquarters wearing a field service cap with battledress!

Folkes is a Midlands solicitor; at a pinch he might just make what is commonly known as the middle class in England. Pale, thin, weakly looking, with semi-thick spectacles, he has all the appearances of an unfortunate clerk who has never seen the sunshine. His light camel-hair greatcoat, in distinction to the proper khaki, makes him conspicuous in the Midland Hotel private bar where, not so long ago, police officers found him after hours. . .

With commendable presence of mind he flourished his 'Security' card that the police and all the semi-intoxicated after-six hangers on might know who he was. And this is the originator of the Don't Talk campaign. Imagine a man receiving his first appointment to a commission, and then in a 'pimping' job, being appointed New Zealand's Himmler. Perhaps it's not so strange. No soldier, no Man, would take on the job.

In pay he is next to Major General Puttick.

The walls have ears

The army does not own Folkes. He is directly responsible to the Prime Minister. In fact the name of Folkes and all his crowd stinks in Army circles. It is not to be wondered at when the private life of every Army officer, what he spends, whether he bets, plays billiards or cards for money, is the subject of attention from Folkes's snoopers in clubs, hotels and elsewhere. Folkes's pimps tap conversations over telephones into and out of Army Headquarters. Privacy is now impossible . . . Every Army officer who opens his mouth these days has to look about first to see if any of Folkes's pimps are about.

Folkes was brought to New Zealand by Colonel Mawhood. He was an acting lieutenant when he left England and became a major while flying across to New Zealand. But no ordinary Major's pay for the Gestapo chief; instead £1,100 a year, and a car for all occasions, business and social.

This outfit of Folkes's costs the country more than £50,000 a year.

Its offices are in the A P A Building, corner of Grey and Featherston Streets, Wellington. With drawn blinds and a sentry at the door it is the essence of secrecy. In fact, so blatantly secret that it is the laugh of the town and specially the tenants of the building.

The People who carry the tales

Second in command of the Gestapo is Lieutenant Cutfield, an ex-hardware shop assistant from Stratford! Selling hardware gives a superior insight into human nature and makes recognition of a spy a certainty.

Another hanger-on in Wellington is Lieutenant Swavely Ellis, one of the 'younger set', who once told the world he would not enlist, but has secured safety with Folkes, despite ballot call-up.

Then there is Second Lieutenant Terence McLean, once an ornament of that influencial highbrow journal, the *Sports Post*. McLean married, too late to be 'married' within the regulations, a daughter of Mr Percy Coyle, secretary of the Licenced Victuallers' Association, and got shoved into camp with early ballotees. But not for long. . . . Folkes considers [him] to be one of his brightest boys. He is a brother of the publicity officer of the National Party, who was once a *New Zealand Observer* editor.

Also at Wellington (there are no privates in Folkes's army – nothing less than a sergeant):

Sergeant Dosser, ex-stud salesman, Wright Stephenson's.

Sergeant Etherington, formerly in charge of advertising for W D and H O Wills [cigarette manufacturers].

Sergeant Nicholls, ex-James Smith mercery department.

Sergeant Rink, ex-passenger agent at Panama.

Sergeant Noble (now commissioned), once parliamentary reporter for *Otago Daily Times*. Enlisted for overseas service. Recommended by Minister of Defence for Officers Training School but army took no notice. Then got leave of absence for domestic reasons and reappeared as one of Folkes's [staff]. . . . Did great work in tapping telephone conversations; another of those spirited out of the NZEF.

Sergeant D H S Taylor, fired from *N Z Truth* and turned his training to good account by joining Folkes. Hard to keep track of – in battledress one day and mufti the next; looks really mysterious.

Sergeant Protheroe, ex-National Broadcasting Service.

Sergeant White, prominent Wellesley Club member and Wellington 'socialite'. Married the daughter of Professor Hunter. Snoops at club on Army Headquarters heads.

Sergeant Douglas, a Wellington importer and agent.

Sergeant Meakin, ex-General Motors.

Miss Molly Bishop, daughter of secretary of N Z Mineowners' Federation. The head of the female section. . . . at social gatherings and poses as member of Navy Office staff.

Miss Joan Young, Public Service Queen in this year's queen carnival, daughter of Director General of Post and Telegraph Department . . .

These young 'ladies' try to put it across unfortunate gallant guards at defence headquarters by stating that they want to go in to see girl friends or relatives. Obliging a lady, the guards get it in the neck when Folkes complains.

At Auckland:

Captain Meikle, formerly Major Meikle of Rifle Brigade.

Four sergeants and one typist.

This office stinks less than the others, possibly because Meikle, being an ex-serviceman, will not stoop as low as Folkes and his stay-at-homes.

Lies, Trickery, Theft

The duties of the S I [Security Intelligence] are to test security measures and this involves trying to get access to wharves, guard posts, etc by pitching tales to police or sentries. Also, theft of keys, documents etc has been resorted to. Witness the occasion when one pimp used his uniform to get into Trentham camp and then stole a bag of papers. Smart work!

There was the famous attempt to trap a suspected spy at the Hotel St George. Four sergeants were installed in the next room and, two by two, stayed there five days. An Otago Varsity student, Bradley, was imported to help. A very secret job, except to the innocent suspect, the hotel staff, and half the town. And then there was the stealthy pursuit of Mr Braun, an American in New Zealand drilling for an oil company.

One of the big jobs is compiling dossiers, written by the staff and their associates, concerning all sorts of individuals. Any of their opinions are recorded in these Gestapo files. What suitable men they are to pass judgement on decent citizens. In addition to their ordinary lack of qualifications, they are misfits, unfits and shirkers. Some of them pitch the tale that they were forced into the job by the Army. Nothing is further from the truth. The two or three who were balloted and found unfit took the job because they preferred pimping to doing a man's job on coast defence or similar duties. They are all in the job because they sought it.

Folkes's wife and family arrived this year from England so he evidently thinks the Gestapo is here to stay. They live at 51 Sefton Street, Wadestown. [A pencilled note added that Mrs Folkes had found a clerical job in the Income Tax Department.]

All the officers have cars with private number plates provided by the State, with unlimited petrol. Home to lunch is the rule. And when Himmler travels far Air Force plane is the transport.

Take this description of the Nazi Secret State Police (Geheime Staatspolizei) and see what difference there is between it and Folkes's outfit:

This organization is responsible for combating any movement subversive to the present regime, and with this object in view keeps constant watch on former members of the Socialist and Communist parties and other political suspects, as well as the constabulary and the rank and file of the National Socialist Party and indeed the whole population. . . .

So, readers of the *People's Voice* were given quite a lot of facts about the Security Intelligence Bureau, mixed with the extreme political view that it was a budding mini-Gestapo similar to its sinister cousin in Nazi Germany.

CHAPTER 6

THE JOVIAL SEA CAPTAIN BY THE NAME OF CALDER

We left Syd Ross (now known as Captain Calder) relaxing in a comfortable sleeping compartment on the Limited Express on the North Island main trunk railway to Auckland, on his way to meet Captain Meikle and his Security Intelligence Branch staff. These security officers will be his new companions to help root out the imagined band of advance German insurgents who were said by Captain Calder to be holed up in the town of Rotorua, planning to attack strategic places in the centre of the North Island, and then, perhaps, advance down to Wellington to assassinate senior government figures and create general mayhem, and even snatch political power.

Readers of this book will know that this sinister band existed only in Ross's imagination, though news of them had spread to a few politicians (who saw parallels with the Australia First movement over the Tasman) and Major Folkes, the Director of Security, who had proved to be particularly drawn to the story, and seems to be advancing his own (very self-interested) agenda.

Ross arrived at Auckland railway station early on Tuesday morning, well rested and looking authoritative in his Merchant Navy uniform, with its peaked cap. He had breakfast, and read the *Herald,* noting news of the round-up of Australia First conspirators in Sydney. From a telephone box he rang Captain Meikle, who had heard from Major Folkes, and was expecting him. He told Calder to take a taxi round to Army HQ, where he had an office, so that they could decide just how he should be deployed.

Ross, the role-player and performer, was equal to that: '*Are you mad?*' he snapped, 'Good God, man . . . I mustn't be seen within a mile of Army HQ. I'd give myself away! *It'll be watched*! What are you thinking of? We've got to meet somewhere safe. Look, I'll ring you back in half an hour when you've sorted things out.'

Later in the morning a rather shamefaced Captain Meikle and another SIB officer, Captain Steven, met their visitor at a hurriedly arranged safe house, and decided that he would be provided with a car and supplied with all the petrol and money he would need to carry out his important mission. To assure his safety and keep tabs on everything, Calder would be followed discreetly by Steven, who would keep notes and report back to Meikle.

No time was wasted, and in a day or two he was equipped, for £200, with a powerful second-hand (but of recent make) Ford V8 coupé – a style of car not often seen these days, but common then, with two doors and a single well-sprung bench front seat for a driver and one or two companions and a luggage compartment in the tail that could be rearranged as a seat for one or two open-air passengers. These cars were not as heavy as Ford V8 saloons with regular back and front seats and four doors, so their performance – particularly acceleration – was better. Just the thing for Calder.

Steven was given plenty of petrol vouchers for both of them, and a wad of money, from which he obligingly peeled pound notes whenever Calder asked for them. Ross soon zoomed off in the direction of Rotorua, while Steven, in a more modest car, and accompanied by his wife to give his journey an innocent look, journeyed more slowly by another route. It was arranged that they would meet that evening by chance at a Rotorua hotel.

At Rotorua Calder easily took on the role of a jovial

sea captain, happy to be at leisure while his vessel was under repair. He joined the local armed services club, and was soon hobnobbing on first-name terms with everyone. He struck just the right mix of a gregarious mariner with a fund of apt stories, and a generous acquaintance who was ever ready to take a friend anywhere he wished in his well-appointed car.

Calder stayed at the Grand, the most comfortable hotel in Rotorua, and on some days drove off on assignations with (as Steven understood it) some of the villains that he was keeping an eye on. When he was away on these mysterious trips he insisted that Steven remain behind 'so that my cover won't be blown', but in the evening he would share notes with him, and suggest leads that Steven should follow up over the next few days.

By these simple expedients Calder set up a chain of deceptions that left him fairly free to do as he liked and have a jolly old time of it. At the same time he kept his SIB minder scurrying about and busy sending off notes to Meikle. These were polished up at the Auckland office and sent to Folkes in Wellington, who embellished them still further before dispatching them to the Prime Minister as part of an agenda he was developing. It was the same formula that had worked well while Calder was in Wellington: a plausible storyteller mixing together in the same tale a mass of simple, easily checked truths with a few falsehoods, and getting the whole basketful accepted as a credible account of what was going on.

A typical episode will illustrate Calder's way of working. After breakfast at his hotel – an elaborate affair of bacon, tomatoes and kidneys or liver (a 'mixed grill') – Calder would confer briefly with his obliging SIB minder and pass to him some items that related to the previous day's visit for Steven to discreetly follow up. Then the two men would mount their respective cars and Calder would speed off one way, and Steven amble off in another.

To follow our illustration, let us suppose that Calder paused at a nearby township (say, Te Puke) and dropped into the general store. There he would engage the proprietor (having noted his name *Johnson* painted over the front door) in some general conversation to pick up trivial scraps of information about him and his business, and notice any physical oddities such as warts, moles and thinning hair, and general tallness or shortness. This small set of chores done, Calder was at leisure for the rest of the day, free to enjoy his car and the spending money that Steven kept peeling off for him.

Of course, the Rotorua area had plenty of attractions to divert a man who had been confined to jail for a few years. The geysers and hot baths, the native bush bejewelled with little lakes and the vast new pine plantations, the sea coast a pleasant hour's drive away. All were plausible places to keep an eye open for German insurgents.

That evening, or the next morning, he would confer with Steven and report on his contact for the day – '. . . met a thick-set fella whose cover is to run the general store there . . . name of Johnson . . . gutteral voice, with a mole on the side of his nose with hairs growing out of it . . . he's a tough character who'll be into a lot of violence when he gets the signal . . .' – and so on.

Over the next day or so Steven would drop into Johnson's store to innocently buy some trivial piece of hardware, and there behind the counter would be a stocky man with a deep voice and a mole on the side of his nose with small hairs sprouting from it. Steven would then retire to his car and record the sighting of yet another treacherous fifth-columnist, this one (positively identified by certain small blemishes on his face) using the cunningly contrived cover of running a general store. Off would go a report to Folkes that yet another traitor had been identified, and a day or two later the Prime Minister would know too.

This example is of course a little simpler than any actual event would have been, but it illustrates the course of events that kept a constant trickle of names of identified 'subversives' flowing from Rotorua to the SIB office in Auckland and then on to Folkes at Head Office in Wellington, and then to the Prime Minister's office in Parliament Buildings.

Inevitably, a few of the names that travelled that route from Rotorua to Parliament Buildings caused a shock when they got there. One of these belonged to an innocent Aucklander by the name of Walter Gilbert Crackles Ashbridge. 'Crackles' was a disarmingly appropriate name for him, because he was a radio operator at the Musik Point radio signals unit in Auckland. This radio transmitting/receiving station was engaged in top secret, strategically significant wartime work.

The unit had been fitted out, before the war, with newly-invented radio direction-finding equipment for keeping safety tabs on civilian aircraft approaching or leaving New Zealand. With the coming of war, some of the staff were given special security clearances and set to work as signals intelligence officers, intercepting morse code enemy radio messages and passing them to code-breakers to crack and analysts to interpret.

Some of the signals that these officers picked up were enciphered or encrypted bursts of morse code transmitted between German surface naval ships and submarines (U-boats) in the Atlantic and their home bases in Germany. The New Zealand station was one element in the worldwide network of over fifty British secret radio stations. It was vital to the web because it was on the other side of the world from the Atlantic, so that it was night here when it was daytime there, and short-wave radio signals are most easily picked up at night.

As one of Nicky Hager's informants on page 275 of his book *Secret Power* (Craig Potton Publishing, 1996) puts it: 'The dark side of the world picks up radio signals better, and so when darkness was across this side of the world we'd get the signals from the German U-boats in the Atlantic. We'd pick them up at Awarua down South [near Bluff], and Musik Point in Auckland, and we would immediately send them on to intelligence headquarters in London and they would take a cross bearing to work out where the submarine was.'

The content of the signal could be of use if it could be deciphered quickly and interpreted, but the immediate job at Musik Point was to find the bearing – the point on the compass – along which the signal came. If a station in another part of the world heard the same signal and also got a bearing, lines could be drawn on a map showing the bearings from both stations, and the U-boat would be located at the point where the two lines crossed. The German could then be tracked between one set of signals and the next to find its location and direction of travel, and aircraft (or ships) could be sent to search for it. . .

Better still, a morse code message from a U-boat might be detected in the Atlantic by a Musik Point receiver focused on signals coming from beyond the Indian Ocean and Africa, and as soon as a bearing was set the same receiver could be swung round to catch the end of the same signal from the east – from away over the Pacific Ocean and North or South America. In that way, Musik Point radio could, at night, sometimes let London have two bearings on a chattering U-boat, and a ship or plane could be sent to search the ocean at the point where the two bearings intersected.

At the very least the signals could be used to keep a tally on the number of enemy submarines operating in the Atlantic and, roughly, the position of each.

It was all very covert work, of course, as the German naval authorities did not know that Allied radio interception was so well organised, and that a night-time vigil for U-boat radio signals was being kept at such a remote place on the other side of the world.

Imagine the dismay in the Prime Minister's office when one of the Security Intelligence Bureau's lists of fifth-columnists turned up with the name of a radio operator from Musik Point on it!

CHAPTER 7

THE POLICE JOIN
THE PLAY

For the following two months or so (April and May 1942) Calder enjoyed a merry holiday. In the mild autumn weather he made up for all those months of irksome confinement at Waikeria, and sped all over the central North Island, even down as far as Wellington and Petone, renewing friendships and making new contacts. To all he was good-natured and obliging – obviously a successful and well-off man with plenty of time to take an interest in everyone he met.

Several times he sped to Auckland to visit his mother, and drop in on old cobbers who were impressed to find their friend transformed as if by magic into a well-connected sea captain. He made new friends and spent a good deal of time ferrying them round to visit their relations. He seemed too good to be true – always so courteous and obliging.

A friend he called on over and over again was an old lag from Waikeria. Charlie Remmers had been imprisoned for forgery and counterfeiting, and by all accounts was an artistic and articulate man, with a down-to-earth kit of dry attitudes and cynical opinions, always ready for a good hearty laugh at authority figures who took themselves seriously.

Ex-prisoners tell of Syd and Charlie often in close conversation while locked up in prison, with bursts of laughter that generally turned on the frailties of men in authority over them – from warders and the prison Governor to the Minister of Justice, and even the Prime

Copy of criminal record listed in the Police Gazette
MC = Magistrates Court SC = Supreme Court

Remmers, Charles Alfred

Born 1889 (England)

Had been a police constable in England.
Fresh complexion, bald (wears wig), brown eyes.
Labourer, builder and motor dealer.

Wellington SC	17.2.13	Breaking, entering & theft	3 years
		Theft (6 charges)	18 months on each
		Discharged on special remission,	
		week ended 6.3.15	

Wellington SC	12.2.32	Conspiracy	Acquitted

False pretences, attempted false pretences
Forgery (8 charges)
Uttering, attempted uttering* (4 charges each)
18 months on each

Wellington SC	18.10.37	Forgery (2 charges)	4 years on each
Auckland SC	19.10.37	Uttering forged banknote	Acquitted on one
		(4 charges)	charge of uttering
		Attempting to utter	1 year on each
		forged banknote	(cumulative)

*uttering = putting forged money into circulation

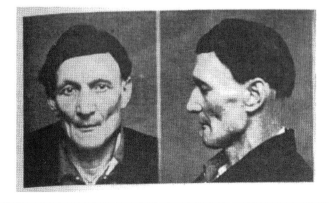

Minister himself (whose characteristic Scots accent Ross could mimic entertainingly). It is easy to see here the germ of an idea for a hoax that one of them was soon to carry off so successfully.

By an odd twist Captain Meikle had heard of Remmers (who was well known to police through a striking mugshot in the *Police Gazette*), and suggested that Calder should keep an eye on him at his home at 9 Boston Terrace, just off Aro Street in Wellington; and at the Rotorua boarding house 'Malfroy Villa' where he sometimes stayed. When Calder caught up with his old prison friend and told him of this SIB suspicion of him they shared the joke and decided that Remmers should act out the subversive part that had been assigned to him by the SIB. So Ross and Remmers continued the close partnership that they had struck up in prison – but now in much happier circumstances and giving them even more fun, with real SIB officers being fooled, and government ministers drawn into the game.

Prompted and urged by his commanding officer in Wellington, Captain Meikle was by now convinced that there was a cell of enemy conspirators at Rotorua. He guessed that these miscreants would have picked the town because it was a tourist centre in which strangers would not be much noticed; and the landlady at Malfroy Villa, opposite the Fire Station, was a Mrs Neuman – *a German* with several boarders *who had foreign names,* and another of whom was Charlie Remmers – a known suspect. And would not the Germans and their supporters be confirmed in their choice of Rotorua by the fact that the police there were the dumbest in New Zealand – as Meikle often commented: a mob who could not even catch a cold? Meikle was spurred on by regular phone calls from his boss Major Folkes in Wellington pressing for news of the Nazi plotters that would be so alarming that the government would be obliged to pass those British

18(b) (Defence Act) regulations to give the SIB power over the Dominion's police – to deal with Nazi conspirators without all the palaver of bringing them before a court. Meikle and Steven saw that it was their duty to come up with the sort of evidence that was wanted.

Unfortunately for the Auckland SIB officers under Captain Meikle's command, the local Rotorua police were about to join in the play, and spoil the whole game. Indeed, by early June they had noticed the tall, brown-headed sea captain who looked remarkably like a certain Syd Ross who was well known to them, and whose photograph was plainly displayed in a recent issue of the *Police Gazette* – and who now seemed to be well off and at leisure, and in control of a powerful up-to-date motor car and any amount of petrol.

Constable J. Richardson of the Rotorua police led off with this internal police message to Detective Constable F.R. Henry (2932) at 11.40 am on 4 June 1942:

```
On two occasions during the past three weeks
a man has stayed at the Grand Hotel, Rotorua,
and represented himself as Captain CALDER,
a Secret Service Agent. He did not mention a
particular branch of the Secret Service.
On the first occasion he came to Rotorua, about
three weeks ago, he was driving a 3-seater
motorcar.
On the second occasion he came to Rotorua,
which was either on 29th or 30th May 1942, he
was driving a greeny-blue 3-seater car.
He left the Grand Hotel at Rotorua at about 2
pm yesterday, 3/6/42, and told Mr Clement COOK,
Licensee of the Grand Hotel, that he was going
to stay with his mother at Auckland (address
not stated) and would return to Rotorua at
about the end of this week.
This man has paid up his accounts at the
Grand Hotel and there is no evidence that he
has committed any offence except, perhaps, a
```

misrepresentation that he is Captain CALDER, a
Secret Service Agent.
The man was dressed in civilian clothes,
wearing a brown coat.
The licensee of the Grand Hotel, Rotorua,
Clement COOK, has identified the photographs
of Sydney Gordon ROSS on P.G. [Police Gazette]
1939 page 73 as those of this man representing
himself to be a Secret Service agent.
I saw Sydney Gordon ROSS, mentioned, in Rotorua
yesterday, 3/6/42.
Inspector CARROLL asks that you relay this
message to Auckland in case the Police there
have inquiries for ROSS or a fictitious Secret
Service Agent.

Further sightings followed:

NEW ZEALAND POLICE
> *Police-Station:* <u>Rotorua</u>
> *Date:* <u>6th, June,</u>   <u>1942.</u>
REPORT of _____ <u>Constable M. Egan,</u> *No.* <u>3366.</u>

relative to <u>Motor Car Licensed No. 139-017 failing to keep</u>
<u>the left at the intersection of Tutanekai and Arawa Street</u>
<u>and fails to stop when signalled by me to do so on Friday</u>
<u>5th, June, 1942.</u>

I respectfully report that at 8.40pm, Friday
5th June 1942 I was on duty at the corner of
Tutanekai and Arawa Streets when I noticed a
motor car, licenced number 139-017, proceeding
along Tutanekai Street travelling north, and
turn to its right into Arawa Street, failing
to keep to the left of the intersection. While
turning the corner the car was eight feet over
the central line on its wrong side.
    I stepped out to stop this car by putting
up my hand but the driver ignored my signal
and kept on going along Arawa Street to-wards

Fenton Street.

The lights of this car were on me when I
signalled and I was in uniform at the time.

I obtained the number of this car as it
passed.

At 5.30 this morning I observed this car
parked outside the Grand Hotel in Fenton
Street. I placed a sticker on the windscreen
requesting the driver to call at the Police
Station as he was being reported for a breach
of the Traffic Regulations.

He did not call and produce the sticker. He
was later brought to this Station regarding
another matter.

He is Sydney Gordon ROSS and is going under
the name of Captain CALDER, staying at the
Grand Hotel.

ROSS is referred to in Police Gazette 1942,
P.337, Photo, 10. 1939, p.73.

Constable Egan   Constable 3366.
For special reasons I am not instructing
a prosecution meantime.

NEW ZEALAND POLICE
                    Police-Station: Rotorua
                    Date: 8th, June,   1942.
REPORT of   Detective Sergeant A.J. White,   *No.* 2599
relative to Sydney Gordon Ross. P.G. 1942/337 and photo
P.G. 1939 page 73 – masquerading as 'Captain Calder'

I respectfully report that on the evening of
the 5th Inst whilst on annual leave I happened
to be at the Police Station. Two men called
shortly before 9 p.m. and made a request to see
me personally.

One of the men informed me that he was
'Captain Calder' and wished to speak to me
privately. The three of us then went into one
of the rooms. The man who said he was Captain
Calder then introduced the other man with him

as Mr Brooker. I asked the man Captain Calder who was in civilian clothes if he had anything on him to identify himself as Captain Calder. Captain Calder then said to me 'What the devil do you mean by asking Cook the Licensee at the Grand Hotel to search my bags'.

As I had not the remotest idea what he was talking about I was rather taken aback with his attitude. I asked him to repeat himself and also explain himself. He then again accused me of requesting Mr Cook the Licensee of the Grand Hotel to search his bags and said that I had given Mr Cook authority in writing to do so.

I told the man Captain Calder that he was talking rubbish and further that I did not know what he was talking about or who he was and wanted him to produce credentials before I would discuss anything with him. Calder then informed me that he and Brooker were engaged by Security Intelligence and that they never carried anything that would disclose their identity. After some further conversation Calder said it was obvious that he had made a mistake about me informing Mr Cook and he apologised and said 'I will get you to have lunch with me at the Grand one day'. Calder and Brooker left me at about 8.45 p.m.

On the morning of the 6th inst I returned to duty in order to investigate this matter further as there appeared to me to be something very peculiar about Captain Calder and his friend Brooker. On making further inquiries I discovered that Captain Calder was identical with Sydney Gordon Ross referred to in P.G. 1942 page 337 and photo P.G. 1939 page 73. With the assistance of Constable McIntosh I located Captain Calder again and interviewed him at the Police Station. I put it to him that he was Sydney Gordon Ross and he said that was quite right but he said he had authority to call himself Captain Calder and was in the employ of Security Intelligence under a Captain Meikle of Auckland. He gave a telephone number 32-071 Auckland which he said was an unlisted secret army number and a ring there would verify his statement.

Prior to seeing Ross I had seen Mr Cook the Licensee of the Grand Hotel about Calder. Cook informed me that he knew that Calder was Ross and that Ross was a convicted criminal. He said that a High Official had told him that Captain Calder was on secret inquiries and not to interfere with him. I asked Mr Cook who the High official was and he said that he could not tell me. I told Mr Cook that it seemed very extraordinary to me that some high official should tell a publican that this man Captain Calder was on some secret service but that the Police in the town were told nothing.

Ross was in possession of a Ford V8 3 seater motor car No 139-017. Ross said the car was his and that he had paid £200 for it. He said that he was supplied with benzine by his employers and that he had 16 gallons in his car at the time. He said he did not have a license for benzine but was supplied with all he required in a special way that he was not prepared to disclose.

I made inquiry and found that the number Ross had given 32-071 Auckland was an unlisted Army number. I rang that number and informed them who was speaking. The man at the other end said he was Gray. I asked him if he knew of a man named Captain Calder at Rotorua. He said 'yes, we know him, wait and I will get Captain Steven to speak to you he knows all about him'. A man then spoke who said he was Captain Steven and wanted to know what the trouble was. I asked him if he knew Captain Calder and he said yes. I asked him if he knew who Captain Calder really was and he said 'Yes I know all about him, what is the trouble'. I informed Steven that Captain Calder

was masquerading under a false name which
was a breach of the Change of Name Emergency
Regulations and I considered that in this case
it was a serious breach.

Steven then asked if we could defer doing
anything until he came to Rotorua and said he
was leaving by car immediately. I asked Captain
Steven if he could bring credentials with him
to prove who he was as I would not accept
him unless he could prove his identity or be
vouched for by some responsible person in the
Army at Rotorua. Steven said he would bring
credentials and arranged to meet me at the
Police Station at 4.30 p.m. that day.

After conferring with Inspector Carroll
on the matter Ross was allowed to go in the
meantime until this man Steven was seen.
During that afternoon I saw Major Laffey and
Colonel Wood at the Military Camp. They were
attending a football match Army v. Air Force.
Major Laffey is known to me personally and I
spoke to him about this matter and asked him
if he knew Captain Calder or Mr Brooker or
Captain Steven. Major Laffey said he did not
know any of them. However Major Laffey said
he could assist me with any credentials that
Steven could produce and inform me if they
were genuine or not. Colonel Wood O.C. of the
Camp at Rotorua knew Calder and while I was
speaking to Colonel Wood Ross himself came
along and started speaking to Colonel Wood
in very friendly and familiar terms. This was
obviously done by Ross for my benefit.

Captain Steven from Auckland came to the
Police Station at 4.30 p.m. as arranged and
he was accompanied by the man Brooker who
was with Ross on the evening of the 5th inst.
Steven produced a card showing that he was
entitled to make any inquiries he required
anywhere and also another card authorising him
to go to any prohibited place and also a note
giving him authority to make inquiries signed

by Captain Meikle of Auckland.

I got Major Laffey to come to the Police Station and examine the credentials and he informed me that they were in order. Steven's photo was on the card and was signed by him. His name is Robert Craig Steven and he is working under Captain Meikle for Security Intelligence at Auckland. The man Brooker comes from Wellington. He informed me that he had similar identification cards to Steven but under instruction he had left them at Wellington. Steven said that he never carried his cards on him only brought them to identify himself to the Police at Rotorua. Captain Steven informed us that he knew Ross and knew of his record and all about him. He said Ross was discharged from prison on the 28th March 1942 and he knew everything that Ross had done from that date. He said that Ross was employed on very important and dangerous work for the State and they did not want him hampered or interfered with. Steven went on to say that if the Police made it known about Rotorua that Captain Calder was a criminal named Ross and was engaged on secret work that Ross's life would be in grave danger. I told Captain Steven that I thought that he was being very melodramatic.

I told Captain Steven I could not see the necessity for Ross masquerading about as Captain Calder, staying at the Grand Hotel and hob-nobbing with the high military and Air Force Officers at Rotorua.

Captain Steven said that Ross was not being paid by them but was being 'used' by them and that he was doing very important work. If Ross is not being paid by them he is getting funds from somewhere as he had been staying at the Grand Hotel on and off since the 15th May and he pays his way and entertains a good deal. He seems to have plenty of money.

Inspector Carroll was present when Captain

Steven and Brooker were at the Station.

At the request of Captain Steven Inspector Carroll decided to allow the matter to rest as it was in the meantime until something further was known.

That evening at the request of Inspector Carroll I rang Inspector Edwards at Hamilton and told him briefly of the position. The Inspector asked that the matter be reported and he would forward it to Wellington. He suggested that we ring Auckland for further verification. I rang Det Sergt Stevenson of Auckland. He informed me that he knew Captain Steven of Security Intelligence. He said that Steven was right hand man to Captain Meikle who was in charge of Security Intelligence at Auckland. Det Sergt Stevenson also knew the telephone number 32-071 Auckland as being an Army telephone number.

I attach hereto a list of Ross's convictions. It seems extraordinary that a man with a criminal list such as Ross has should be allowed to masquerade as a Captain and live at the leading Hotel and mix with high Army and Air Force officers. On learning who Captain Calder was I was greatly concerned that this criminal should be in our midst masquerading as he was.

When Ross spoke to Colonel Wood in my presence on the 6th inst he told the Colonel that he had received word that his niece had died in Auckland and he showed the Colonel a telegram. Colonel Wood later informed me that the telegram said 'Come home Monday if Possible, Mum' or words to that effect.

Later Captain Steven informed me that he had told Ross of the death of his niece when he arrived at Rotorua.

I am informed that Ross left Rotorua yesterday but is expected to return. It seems to me as if the death of the niece and the telegram have been rigged to withdraw Ross from

Rotorua on account of Police interest in Ross.
It seemed peculiar to me that Steven should
bring Ross the news of the death of a niece at
this juncture.

I might state here that Colonel Wood did
not know that Captain Calder was Sydney
Gordon Ross a criminal. He knows now. I am
greatly concerned about this criminal being in
Rotorua and masquerading about as a Captain
Calder. A definite breach of the Change of Name
Regulations has been committed and Ross is
being placed in a position where he can gain
valuable information to assist him in any
criminal activities.

Captain Steven said he would vouch for
Ross while he was working for him and he
expected that he would be engaged on his
present work for another six weeks. Captain
Steven also vouched for Brooker. Brooker came
from Wellington. He said he was a Solicitor
in Wellington. He is attached to Security
Intelligence at Wellington. I do not know any
particulars about him. He is about 35 years,
5ft 7in, dark and well built.

Captain Steven was very anxious that this
matter should not be made the subject of any
report at the present time. He wanted us to
leave the matter as it was and not put in
any reports as he stated that if too many
got to know about Ross's activities it would
be dangerous to Ross and may make a vital
difference to National Affairs. I told Steven
that I was making a full report on the matter
whether he liked it or not. I also told him
that I considered they had very peculiar ways
of going about things and ways that I did not
approve of.

I was by no means impressed by Captain
Steven or the man Brooker who was with him.
Ross of course we know to be a criminal. If
the security of the Country or the State is in
the hands of men such as Steven, Brooker and a

criminal like Ross the outlook for the Country
or the State is not very bright.

For your information please.

A. J. White
Detective Sergeant

NEW ZEALAND POLICE

Subject: <u>Sydney Gordon Ross, P.G. 1942/337 under notice
at Rotorua as an alleged secret service agent.</u>

The Inspector of Police,
    Hamilton.
    For your information. Major Folkes has Ross
employed in his service, but in what capacity
I do not know. He should be kept under close
and secret observation, as he has a motor
car, plenty of benzine, and is obviously well
supplied with money when he can stay at the
Grand Hotel, Rotorua. He is the very type of
man that one would expect to commit a crime
and at the same time pretend to be detecting
or watching for some person or persons
committing the crime that he intended to
commit himself. The fact that Ross is in the
employ of the Security Intelligence Section
of the Army should be kept a close secret. If
a crime is committed where he is located, he
should not be overlooked as a likely suspect.
                    D.J. Cummings
10/6/1942.   Commissioner

The Inspector
    Rotorua.
    For your information please.
            G.B. Edwards
12/6/42   Inspector of Police, Hamilton.

```
Detective Sergeant White
  Please note and report in due course
accordingly.
        G. Carroll
        Insp.
        18/6/42

The Inspector
  Respectfully noted.
        A.J. White
        Det. Sgt.
        18/6/42

The Inspector of Police, Hamilton.
  Noted please.
        G. Carroll
        Insp.
        18/6/42

The Commissioner
  Noted and returned.
        G.B. Edwards
        Inspector of Police, Hamilton.
```

Things were coming unstuck in Wellington too.

Some of Calder's trips took him to Auckland, where he generally called at SIB Headquarters (after dark, to avoid being seen) to report on his surveillance work. A report we have of one of these visits shows his skills as an intriguing entertainer, holding the attention of a handful of off-duty officers with an odd piece of simple maths that, he suggested, would interest their children and give them something to question their schoolteachers about.

The puzzle he put to them was to look again at any simple addition sum, as, for instance, $168 + 397 = 565$, that is

$$168$$
$$\underline{397}$$
$$\underline{565}$$

The twist was to expose a curious result when he added the individual figures horizontally, like this:

168   1 + 6 + 8 = 15 then 1 + 5 = 6

397   3 + 9 + 7 = 19 then 1 + 9 = 10 and 1 + 0 = 1 $\Big\}$ and 6 + 1 = 7

565   5 + 6 + 5 = 16 then 1 + 6 = 7

So, the two top lines have extended to deliver the combined total figure 7, which is the same total that the third line extends to: 7. He showed that this odd result was true for all addition and subtraction sums.

It looks like a typical Ross party trick from his past, and shows the convivial relaxed times that Ross spent in the Auckland office. The performer entertaining again!

However, a later visit to SIB Headquarters in early June was not to be so relaxed and occupied with trivia, for he found Meikle and Steven deep in anxious conference and learned that the idyll of the past couple of months was in danger of being shattered. The trouble turned out to be that the stream of worrying news about German invaders and New Zealand collaborators that was reaching the Prime Minister in Wellington had caused him to reconsider his undertaking to keep the New Zealand police out of the case. Perhaps Mr Fraser had become suspicious of the lists of suspect New Zealanders that were reaching him from Major Kenneth Folkes, his Director of Security, together with increasingly urgent requests to impose Regulation 18(b) that would, in effect, put some important parts of the governance of New Zealand in the Major's hands.

This unwelcome promise of involvement by Police Headquarters added to the irritating enquiries that were coming from local Rotorua police, and being fielded by Meikle, Steven and Brooker. To reassure themselves that they really were engaged on work of national importance the SIB officers gathered round the several large books of clippings and notes that were Auckland SIB's record of the supposed German threat (identical copies of these books – all indexed and tabulated – were kept in Folkes's office in Wellington, and it seems that a third copy was growing steadily in the Prime Minister's office). Calder now saw the Auckland compendium for the first time, and flicked through it, and then returned at once to look more carefully because what he saw was so astounding!

Good grief! How could this be? The books contained his inventions in full – all his visits to pretended subversives, and the detailed accounts of his supposed conversations with them, were all there all right – but these genuine Calder notes comprised only about a third of the entries. The other two-thirds were added by other hands – *but whose hands?*

A good look at the bulky scrapbooks showed that several SIB officers, including some in Wellington, had entered into the spirit of Calder's sport by elaborating the cases he had started, and added a flood of fresh episodes of their own. The entries were no longer a record of his trips and observations (that readers of this book know to be fraudulent) but were now chiefly from others along the same lines, but going much further, with the apparent purpose of proving a pressing danger that could be met only by the extreme action of dissolving civil government and putting New Zealand in the hands of the armed forces, under the guidance of the Security Intelligence Bureau!

Now the fat was in the fire. Calder was astonished to find that his simple hoax had taken on a life that was far beyond anything he had thought of, that might lead him into, well . . . *real trouble.* He stamped about declaring loudly that the whole thing was 'not on the level', while Meikle and Steven worried to see the whole house of cards that they had worked so enthusiastically to build was now being shaken vigorously. Could it stand up?

What was likely to happen next?

At this awkward point I quote directly from an account written by Calder (whose name had by then reverted to Ross) on 2 August 1942 . . .

. . . I was amazed when Captain Meikle informed me that it was the intention of the Prime Minister to bring the Police Department into this business. I asked him why the hell he was not exercising his power. He told me he could not prevent this. He told me still not to worry as he has sufficient pull to prevent the Police from ever coming in . . . **that the whole thing was to get powers 18(b) passed and thus get control of this country in a military manner** . . . I was informed at this stage as I had been informed before, that they had power of control over the Police Department and that the Police took orders from them and therefore the Police could not make any charges, and that the Police would not be brought into this matter at any stage at all . . .

At this stage he [Meikle] made a hurried trip to Wellington where he had a long conference with Major Folkes . . . in the meantime I had been to Rotorua but returned to Auckland when Meikle returned from Wellington. I interviewed Meikle at his home in Minehaha Avenue, Takapuna. He struck me as being an extremely worried man and informed me that the Prime Minister decided to bring the Police into the affair at the finish, but he said that Major Folkes had discovered a way out which would prevent the Police from coming in. He said that they were going to bring the Americans into it, and that they would bring power to bear on the Police Department which would prevent them taking any steps at all in the matter . . .

At this stage I became a trifle worried myself. I was also losing a lot of faith in these so-called powers which Meikle and Folkes were alleged to have possessed. I suggest to Meikle that he was to tell Folkes that by bringing the Americans in to prevent the Police from taking any steps he was jumping from the frying pan into the fire, as he would find the Americans every bit as difficult to convince on the articles contained in the volumes [scrapbooks] as the Police Department would be. At this stage I could see that the members of the Gestapo [Ross's name for the SIB] were in a desperate plight. After having perused these volumes I can now understand just how their plight was so desperate, because the stuff contained in these volumes is about one page of material that I supplied, to three pages of fiction made up by the Security Department.

However, Meikle persisted in carrying out Folkes's instructions and bringing the Americans into it. The following day the man from the American Intelligence Department was interviewed by Meikle in Meikle's office in Auckland. It appears that the interview did not turn out favourably to the New Zealand Gestapo, as they frankly admitted immediately after
. . .

CHAPTER 8

CLIMAX – AND THINGS COME ADRIFT

Readers of this unlikely, but true, story will see that the great adventure that began as a hoax hatched by two bored prison inmates – a forger and a prankster/conman at Waikeria prison in the centre of the North Island of New Zealand – has now run its course, and should by rights be exposed and wound up to the discomfort of several senior figures, including the Prime Minister and the Minister of Public Works, and the consequent glee of many New Zealanders.

But this inevitable climax to the hoax has been complicated and postponed by the astonishing antics of the head of the New Zealand Security Intelligence Bureau, a senior official, second in salary only to Major Puttick in the New Zealand-based military establishment. Major Kenneth Folkes has hijacked the hoax and given it a much more ambitious purpose: to startle the government into pitching the country onto an emergency war footing by enacting a set of regulations based, he believed, on 18(b) of the Defence Act of Great Britain, that would pass wide constitutional powers to the Security Intelligence Bureau, with Folkes at its head.

Folkes and a handful of his senior officers thought it scandalous that the Prime Minister 'lacked the guts' to take that step that would smarten up New Zealand's act '. . . but what can you expect from a government that is just a band of bloody wharfies . . . how much better it would be if Mr Gordon Coates and his crowd were running things ... surely he would see the point of regulation 18(b)!'

And now, horror of horrors, Folkes and Meikle and other SIB officers saw that the whole house of cards that they had worked so hard to build might now be probed by a crowd of flat-footed coppers, with their notebooks and stubby pencils, chasing after hard evidence that was not going to be any help to bounce the government down the 18(b) path.

Indeed, the despised New Zealand police were finding out about both Syd Ross's hoax and Major Kenneth Folkes's conspiracy – from a succession of reports from police officers in the central North Island, and, quite separately, from calls from the Prime Minister to the Commissioner of Police, Mr Cummings, to look into a whole lot of scarcely credible reports that were being sent to him by the head of the Security Intelligence Bureau – from the same parts of New Zealand and sometimes about the very same people.

These two closely related streams were meeting on the desk of the Commissioner of Police, who had by now a pretty good idea of what was going on, and was bracing himself to deliver a swift and devastating kick that would end the independent Security Intelligence Bureau and the bizarre ambitions of its commanding officer.

For Folkes, desperate times called for desperate measures, so he pinned his hopes on two last ditch episodes that, he was sure, would tip the Prime Minister to his way of thinking. First, he would invent some secret intelligence to show that at a known date in the near future there would be a landing on the Kapiti coast of more enemy invaders, to reinforce the handful already supposed to be holed up in Rotorua, under observation by his Captain Calder.

Second, he would put it about that the police had been too free with the news of Syd Ross's connection with the

SIB, so that the Nazi conspirators had learned of it and set about capturing and assassinating him and burying his remains – a just end for a double agent.

An urgent announcement by Folkes to ignite the first of these episodes raised little interest in the armed services, though the police did a little more and made some phone calls to set officers to watch the beaches for hostile landings. A police car travelled north from Wellington calling on local constables and checking beaches to look out for any signs of trouble – flashing lights from seaward, perhaps, or maybe cars facing out to sea, signalling with their headlights. In the event one car, with two people (one an Italian fisherman) in it was spotted facing that way. The occupants were questioned, but were found to be 'engaged in an amatory affair'.

That left Folkes's final scenario – with the forlorn hope that reports of an attempted assassination and burial of Syd Ross would jolt the Prime Minister into action. Ross's cooperation was needed for this drama, so his description of what happened tells the story:

> I left Auckland that evening in the vicinity of four o'clock and made my way to Rotorua. On the way through I procured a spade at an ironmongery shop on the right just after leaving Papakura. I also bought a few feet of rubber tubing for siphoning the benzine out of my tank. Meikle was under the impression that I was to arrange something which looked like an attempt on my life.
>
> On my arrival at Rotorua I spent a few days at Ngongotaha at REMMER's and then proceeded out to the Mamaku Road and went into the bush and dug what was alleged to have been a grave. Immediately after digging the grave — this was on Sunday, 12th July — I hid the spade in the adjoining undergrowth. This has since been recovered from the bush by me in the presence

of a Police Officer and handed to the Police
Department. I then made various marks on my
back with a piece of wet rope to give the
thing some colour that I had been attacked.
I slept in my car that night and immediately
when day broke the following morning, Monday,
13th July [1942], I proceeded, walked, along
the Mamaku Road towards Rotorua where I found
a farm house a few hundred yards off the road
occupied by people called DAHLIN. I saw a young
man there by the name of GUSTAV JOSEPH DAHLIN,
a returned soldier in the present war. He took
me to his shack adjoining the farm house. At
this time I had a coat and singlet on, but
I was minus my shirt and collar and tie. I
told him I was very ill and was a member
of the secret service and I told him it was
absolutely essential that I got in touch with
our Department at Rotorua. I wrote him a note
with a plan . . . and the names STEVEN and
BROOKER on it and told him to take this note
to Pukuatua Street and to give it to Steven
or Brooker. I told him to procure a taxi and
I gave him £1 and as taxis are pretty dear I
gave him another £5 and told him to bring the
change. The next I heard from the Gestapo was
when they arrived at the farm house on Tuesday
morning about 11 o'clock. BROOKER, STEVEN,
NICOLL, Wing Commander NICHOL, Dr. CUDDY
arrived. Dr. CUDDY examined me at the house.
Sergeant NICOLL carried me down from the house.
On the way down I told Brooker and Steven what
had taken place. Steven was very surprised,
Brooker did not show much surprise. He knew it
was coming off. Brooker and Steven then got me
to go up in the car driven by Steven and show
them just where this place was. They went in
and saw the grave. I also showed him where the
car was which was within a couple of hundred
yards from the grave on a deviation part of
the main Rotorua-Hamilton road.

 We then proceed to Pukuatua Street. I had a

bath and went to bed. Steven immediately got
on the phone to Auckland about noon on Tuesday,
14th July. Steven rang Meikle and informed him
what had happened. He told him that an attempt
had been made on my life and things were
pretty bad. Meikle said he was coming down to
see me. Meikle rang Wellington and then rang
Steven again and told him that Folkes was flying
from Wellington the next day.

It would be about 8 p.m. when Meikle arrived
at Rotorua and came to the house in Pukuatua
Street where Meikle, Steven, Brooker and
Sergeant Nicoll were staying. He occupied one
of the back rooms. All the members of the
Gestapo had automatic revolvers and ammunition
in their possession. The revolvers and
ammunition were in a drawer in my room.

On Meikle's arrival he immediately came in
and asked me how I was. The door was shut and
Meikle and I were the only two in the room.
I told him I was O.K. and he said that it
appeared by what he had heard that I had put
the last part over very well indeed. He told
me that Major Folkes was coming up by plane
and he said that he was also sorry to say that
the Assistant Commissioner of Police CUMMINGS
and several detectives were also arriving in
Rotorua. He said they would be down to see
me that night. He said if they came I was to
pretend I was ill and have nothing whatever
to say to them, to even go as far as to
state that I had instructions from the Prime
Minister to say nothing whatever to them.

Shortly after this Meikle got a ring on the
phone which seemed to come from Mr Cummings
to say that they would not be around to see
me until the morning . . . Captain Meikle and
Brooker came into the room and they talked
for several hours on the attitude I was to
adopt when the Police arrived in the morning.
They said that the Assistant Commissioner, Mr
Cummings, was nothing but a bloody big bluff

with a couple of hands like hams and that he would most likely rush into the room . . . and that under no circumstances was I to tell him anything, that I was to stick to the story in the [scrap]books.

The following morning Dr CUDDY came in to see me and examined me. Dr CUDDY asked me for the story of the alleged injuries and I said to him that I was working for the Security Department and there appeared to be jealousy between the New Zealand Gestapo and the Police Department and I did not tell him any more.

Shortly after this Mr Cummings, accompanied by Det.Sgt. Walsh and Det.Sgt. Nalder came into my room. I was asked to get up and go to the Police Station. This I refused to do. I was told by Meikle that the Police were not to question me under any circumstances and I was to stick to my story and have nothing to do with them, as they persisted nothing on earth was to shake me from the story contained in the [scrapbook] volumes. This was arranged with Meikle. When the Police asked me to go to the Station with them and talk the thing over I refused to do so. Mr Cummings then pointed out that the case had been placed in his hands by the Prime Minister which I told him I did not believe and Mr Cummings then offered to ring the Prime Minister in my presence, so at this stage I decided the best thing to do was to go along to the Police Station, still under the impression that Meikle and Folkes would not let the thing come to a head. I was satisfied from what Meikle, under Folkes' direction, told me that they would be strong enough to keep the Police out and not let them in the know. They were not to get the inside workings of these volumes.

I definitely know that there are three sets of volumes in existence. They were in Meikle's possession when I was last in Auckland. They have the photographs and other plans in them.

They offered me one copy of the volume but
I said I would wait until the inquiry was
further advanced. One copy of the volume went
into Folkes' hands.

I got up out of bed, had a cup of tea, and
went down to the Police Station. Before I left
I asked Mr Cummings if I could see Meikle
privately. This was granted, and on Captain
Meikle's arrival in my room I asked him what
the bloody hell was the game, and he said for
me to simply stick to the story in the volumes
and nothing would be done providing I stuck to
the statement contained in the volumes.

I left at this stage for the Police Station
and spent the remainder of the day there with
Det.Sgt. Walsh and Nalder going through my
tours of the North Island followed in nearly
every case by Steven.

Although I told Meikle that I would stick
to the story entirely contained in the volumes
the time I gave Meikle this promise I did not
actually know what I was running myself in
for as the story contained in the volumes was
vastly different and contained a vast amount of
material that was not given to them by myself.
However, I stuck to my bargain with Meikle and
kept to the story throughout the day.

About six o'clock in the evening Meikle
called and picked me up and took me round to
Pukuatua Street. On arrival there I had a cup
of tea and then asked if Folkes had arrived
in Rotorua. Meikle informed me that he had
and I asked him why the hell he was not there
at Pukuatua Street as I wanted to see him
immediately.

At this stage Meikle got on the phone to the
Grand Hotel and got in touch with Major Folkes.
I could hear him talking to him and hear
the conversation. It was quite simple to see
that Folkes was badly scared and although he
promised faithfully that he would fix things up
he did not come round and see me at Pukuatua

Street. Meikle and Brooker spent from then on until 3 o'clock in the morning talking of just what attitude I was to adopt with the Police when they called for me again the following morning. They told me to stick out till 12 o'clock noon and they would then call for me and say they were arresting me under the Military law and take me to Auckland where I would be released and the whole thing would be finished with.

I was very surprised when shortly after my arrival at the Police Station Captain Meikle, on Major Folkes' instructions – Folkes not being man enough to come and do it himself – entered the room in the company of Mr Cummings and two or three detectives and informed me that my services with the New Zealand Gestapo had reached an end and I must consider myself in the same position I was in prior to joining them. He also asked me to sign the car which I had in my possession back to the Gestapo. I said I would place no difficulty in their way concerning the car. I was rather surprised at this attitude, but when Meikle walked to the door he turned round and winked at me. Meikle then left the building and that is the last I ever saw of him or any more of the Gestapo.

Shortly after 12.30 I began to realise that the Gestapo had decided to run out on me as things had got too hot for them. It looked as though they intended to leave me to bear the brunt of things and this made me very angry indeed. I asked Det.Sgt. Nalder did he know where Folkes and Meikle had gone to. He told me he had no idea where they had gone. I told him that if that was the case and they did not turn up before 1.30 there would be some dirty linen washed in the afternoon.

At 2 o'clock when there was no sign of the Gestapo I asked to see Mr Cummings. He came into the room and I decided to tell him the true story concerning the whole affair. Mr

```
Cummings then handed me different volumes
which were alleged to have been composed by
me and I saw at once that it was less than
one-third of the data in these volumes which
was only my story and the other two-thirds
was made up by the Gestapo as the members
of the Gestapo were all keen on getting
further promotion and they wanted something
sensational to give it a boost. What annoyed
me was the paragraph referring to the Prime
Minister in volume 2, page 195. I have read
this paragraph. This was never mentioned by me
and this was a good bit of their propaganda
during the whole of my connection with them.
Brooker was the main spokesman on this thing.
    I wrote a letter to the Prime Minister
saying that I was not associated with the
paragraph mentioned and I posted this letter
at the Rotorua Post Office at 5 o'clock on
Thursday, 16th July in the presence of Det.Sgt.
Nalder and Det.Sgt. Walsh and the car driver.
I addressed the letter to the Right Hon. Mr
Fraser, Prime Minister, Wellington and I marked
'Personal' up on the top left hand corner of
the letter. The letter was stamped and actually
placed in the Post box in the Rotorua Post
Office by me.
```

Police Commissioner Cummings may have got to the bottom of the astonishing hoax being acted out by Syd Ross, and have a pretty good idea of the closely related but much more serious delinquencies of Major Folkes, the government's trusted head of military security. But how to bring the matter to a head, swiftly and efficiently – to wind up Syd's hoax and eliminate entirely the SIB as a body independent of the police?

No trace has been left on the police files that I have seen to show how it was done, but events leave just one scenario that accounts for what happened next.

CHAPTER 9

TRUTH GETS DEEPLY INVOLVED

As New Zealand's Commissioner of Police came to grips with the extraordinary matters that Ross's hoax had thrown up he commented more than once that the plot he was uncovering 'read like a Dennis Wheatley novel'. That was a perceptive comment, and if Ross or Remmers had been regular novel readers it might well have been guessed that Wheatley was the wellspring of their ideas. Wheatley's lucidly written, racy novels, in which audacious heroes had wartime adventures that were a little larger than life, were hugely popular all through the 1940s. The Commissioner's comments were right because Wheatley had personal and family links with the security intelligence community in Britain, and all sorts of surprising acquaintances, such as the traitor 'Lord Haw Haw' who later broadcast regularly from wartime Berlin. Years later, in his autobiography, Wheatley dropped the fact, unknown to him at the time, that the Germans considered appointing him Gauleiter (the local Nazi supremo) of London when they finally won the war. For the Allied side, as a loyal Brit, he pestered the Admiralty in London to abandon transporting vital wartime supplies across the Atlantic in cargo ships grouped in convoys and protected by a ring of warships to ward off enemy submarines, surface raiders and aircraft. Why not, asked Wheatley, ship the stuff more safely on huge U-boat-proof unsinkable barges or rafts made roughly out of unsinkable pine logs bound into rafts and pulled by tugs? Obviously Wheatley was an imaginative man who could have enjoyed turning Ross's escapade (if ever he heard of it) into a novel.

Commissioner Cummings could deal with Ross right enough, but Major Folkes was another matter. The Major was an intense man with a burning conviction that New Zealand urgently needed those services that he was ready to give. He knew that there was a lot to be gained by disciplining the country under his rock-hard fist, even if there was a price to pay – like putting fripperies such as civil liberties on hold.

And if the Axis threat of sabotage and assassination up and down the North Island was not yet quite firm enough to require that extreme step of visiting 18(b), then he, Kenneth Folkes, would set to work and produce the evidence that was needed to harden it up.

Looked at another way, Major Folkes and some of his men were organising an act of subversion, by which he and a few of his army intelligence officers were busy manufacturing a threat, while Folkes pressed the Prime Minister for powers to deal with it. It was a conspiracy to jolt the government into passing some very significant powers from the elected government and regular administration of law and justice, and vest them in a small junta. Of course, the plan was at odds with the practical realities of the day and was driven by just one officer, so had no chance of success. The government had a firm grip on political power and had the loyalty of the police and the armed services.

Police Commissioner Cummings therefore had a delicate task, to end the Ross prank, and at the same time end the power of the head of New Zealand's Security Intelligence Bureau who was acting so eccentrically . . . It would be awkward to charge Folkes, a senior army officer, with breaking the law by inventing a national crisis and then proposing a self-serving remedy to deal with it himself. And anyway, shouldn't the matter be dealt with under military law – by a court martial? How to proceed?

I am bound to say that I have no direct evidence of what happened next, but events that followed admit of only one credible scenario . . . that the Commissioner must have put together a dossier of papers about the Ross hoax, and caused it to be passed covertly to the editor of the weekly newspaper *New Zealand Truth*. At all events, *Truth* was suddenly very well informed about many details on the surface of the Ross affair, with a story written from the New Zealand police point of view, showing the force to be a wonderfully efficient and flexible body that had quickly detected Ross's cheeky fraud and put a stop to it. The compiler of the leaked documents kept the political scandal that was raised directed straight at Major Folkes, and isolated as far as could be from the Prime Minister – as it has stayed ever since. (There is not a scrap about either Ross, Folkes or Captain Calder in Michael King and Michael Bassett's detailed biography of Peter Fraser, *Tomorrow Comes the Song – a life of Peter Fraser,* Penguin, 2000.)

Truth's billboard for 29 July 1942 told the story up and down the country, and page 11 gave the details – which are reproduced as an illustration on pages 94–95.

Shock! Revelation! Amazement! How could such things happen? No doubt Ross floated on a cloud of fulfilment and relief as his successful hoax was brought to a fitting climax . . . Folkes and his supporters must have suffered a nasty shock as their reputations shrank on the instant from trained specialist officers to gullible nitwits. Most New Zealanders who read that issue of *Truth,* or learned the story from someone who did, had a good laugh at the turn of events, and, if it fitted their style, added the Folkes affair to their list of anecdotes and conversation-openers.

(The day after the story was made public, with Major

Security Police Badly Hoaxed

BY IMPUDENT GAOLBIRD

"CAPT. CALDER" EXPOSED

THE OUTSPOKEN people of Australia were recently roused to angry comment on the Public Relations Department (an intelligence organisation) whose activities earned an unprecedented public rebuke from no less eminent a judicial authority than Dr. H. V. Evatt, the Attorney-General.

BUT JUST what the people of New Zealand are going to think about the Security Intelligence Department, a special body of individuals entrusted with the internal security of the Dominion when they are confronted with the gigantic hoax perpetrated by an ex-gaolbird in recent weeks, should be somebody's business.

PEDDLING a fantastic story of his discovery of an alleged plot to assassinate two Cabinet Ministers, while an unwilling guest of His Majesty at Waikeria, this ex-convict gained the confidence of the security police and was sent off to Rotorua to live a life of luxury in the thermal regions.

NOT UNTIL hundreds of pounds of public money had been spent at the instigation of this arch-imposter, was the fantastic official masquerade terminated. Then as the result of the observations of an alert young constable who had committed the rogues' gallery to memory, the civil police, as on other occasions, took a hand and blew wide open the smartest piece of confidence work ever attempted in the Dominion.

APART from the comic aspect of this monstrous bluff, it has a very serious side. First, the manner in which the security department was so blatantly hoodwinked strongly suggests that it is high time its personnel was subjected to a rigorous overhaul.

SECONDLY, while such an organisation may be required for the protection of State and Government in wartime, the public are also entitled to protection from the accusations and suggestions made by any dangerous rascal who may succeed in foisting his services upon this department.

Thirdly, the authorities should see that any secret dossier or reports compiled as a result of the Rotorua exploits of this rascally imposter, and which may reflect on or mention the names of innocent people are instantly destroyed under police supervision.

For some weeks past, the people of Rotorua and district have been seething with the story of the mysterious comings and goings of security intelligence officials. Now that there has been a showdown, they are indignant about the whole thing.

Released from prison at the end of March, this impudent crook was interviewing a Cabinet Minister in Wellington the following day, according to "Truth's" information. As a result of the interview, he was referred to another Minister, whom he told that while he was in prison, German agents had communicated with him and enlisted his services.

Then, obviously, to create greater confidence, the ex-gaolbird told the second Minister of a plot to assassinate him and a colleague. Quite certain that he could be of use to the State, if he acted as undercoverman, while working with the phantom enemy agents, he placed himself at the disposal of the authorities.

The Minister arranged for the ex-convict to be referred to an officer of the security organisation, who swallowed the bait, hook, line and sinker, with the result that the crook became a member of the secret service, vested with all the far-reaching powers that go with membership, notwithstanding the fact that he frankly admitted he had a criminal record.

Given a generous expense allowance, a powerful American car and authority to draw almost unlimited supplies of petrol, the new member of the security organisation installed himself in the Grand Hotel, Rotorua, under the pseudonym of "Captain Calder."

Fortunately for the honor of the Army, this dirty crook was not given a military uniform, or at least did not dare to wear one while bathing under public gaze.

From time to time, "Captain Calder" was away from Rotorua for considerable periods, and almost as regularly, sent his chief a series of colorful and sensational reports of alleged developments. He reported localities, plans and personages supposedly involved in a complex sabotage and invasion project, and gave highly circumstantial accounts of interviews and talks he had had with several people.

Sucking the bait with avidity, the security organisation were in high feather at the Hollywoodenish activities of their new super-sleuth.

A security police big-wig is reported to have actually flown to Rotorua by special plane on several occasions to discuss progress and plans with the priceless "Captain Calder," who must have been bursting his sides with the way the security big boys were swallowing his "disclosures."

IT IS EVEN STATED THAT THIS COOL CARD PERSUADED HIS AUGUST SUPERIORS TO TAKE AERIAL PHOTOGRAPHS OF CERTAIN SPOTS. FOR ALL THE USE THEY WERE, THEY MIGHT JUST AS WELL HAVE PHOTOGRAPHED WHAKA FROM THE AIR OR TRIED TO PHOTOGRAPH THE ODORS THAT ARISE FROM GEYSERLAND!

Always a few jumps ahead of his superior, "Captain Calder" lived a life of luxury for over three months when a young constable unmasked him and promptly reported the matter to his superior.

INQUIRIES THEN REVEALED THAT THE DASHING "CAPTAIN" WHO HAD CARVED A NICHE FOR HIMSELF IN THE SECRET SERVICE OF THE DOMINION, WAS JUST A CHEAP CROOK.

EXPLODED

Finally, the position became so bad that the matter found its way into the hands of the Police Department. Some of the best detective officers in the Dominion, comprising Senior-Detectives A. M. Harding, P. J. Naider and P. Doyle (Wellington), and Senior-Detective J. Walsh (Auckland), directed by the ablest criminal investigator the N.Z. police force has produced in the last quarter century, Superintendent James Cummings, went to Rotorua to unravel the gigantic plot discovered by "Captain Calder."

Two days later, they returned to their respective stations, having proved conclusively that the arch-plotter was "Captain Calder" himself, and that his "startling discoveries" were just the product of a fertile mind bent on making some easy cash without working for it.

Needless to say, "Captain Calder" has been relieved of his appointment after having a wonderful time at the expense of the Dominion's war effort, and two houses costing a pretty penny, which were established as a part of the scheme of things in "Calder's" head, were closed down.

It is conceivable that the two hard-headed Ministers were in no frame of mind to toy with "Calder's" disclosure of plans for their assassination, and handed him over to someone else in order to ascertain whether he was a lunatic, liar or genuine.

Had he just been released from an internment camp where the inmates are openly hostile, he MIGHT have learned something of a wild-cat scheme to shoot persons representing authority that MIGHT have been worth investigating.

Even if "Captain Calder" succeeded in hoodwinking the security officials with highly circumstantial tales of plans for assassinations he would have been quickly run to earth had those most intimately concerned had a little more faith in responsible police officers who have spent a lifetime rounding up and sorting out crooks of "Calder's" ilk; and who (amongst the real top-notchers at any rate) will, in "Truth's" opinion, hold their own with the best in the Empire, in spite of a cumbersome system and poor facilities and equipment.

This incident emphasises the apparent need for an investigation and overhaul, where necessary, of the security organisation before there is a repetition of these blunders and the attendant orgy of jitterbug spending.

But apart from all this, there is a serious danger that innocent people (as they turned out to be in this case) may suffer appalling damage and be the victims of a grave miscarriage of justice, when the security organisation, fooled up to the hilt by a crook, employs him on work which should be done by a man of the highest personal integrity.

It will be iniquitous if any secret dossiers compiled from the information supplied by "Calder" are not destroyed forthwith, because the merest suggestion that a person has been under the surveillance of the security police, may damn him in the eyes of his fellow citizens.

After this latest display of melodramatic fatuity, if the authorities still feel that it is necessary to maintain a security organisation separate from the Police Department, which has earned the respect of the community over a long period of years, it is to be hoped that greater use will be made of men with sound experience in these matters. What are required are New Zealanders with solid commonsense and alert minds, who will not fall for the fantastic humbug of the first glib-tongued imposter who comes along with a story that even a Hollywood scenario writer would turn his nose up at.

Folkes well and truly disgraced, the whole interesting matter was abruptly put beyond discussion in print as New Zealand's press censor forbade further references to the Security Intelligence Bureau and to Syd Ross's hoax.)

Truth was the right paper to carry the story. It was an independent national weekly with a wide circulation, serving as a robust foil to the country's handful of rather dull, conservative daily broadsheet newspapers. *Truth* was a tabloid with striking headlines that were often printed in magenta on the front page, and an editorial staff that had a good understanding that real news stories are the ones that some people in high places would rather not see published at all. At its best it was lively and entertaining as it exposed a succession of wayward clerics and scoutmasters, dishonest businessmen and bumbling public servants, and, of course, a never-ending parade of misbehaving spouses and other petty miscreants.

The story of Syd Ross and the way he fooled New Zealand's Director of Security and gained for himself a merry holiday at the taxpayer's expense was right up *Truth*'s alley. A lovely simple story – 'crim cons head of security and lives the life of Reilly until the cops inevitably catch up with him'.

Truth broke the news and brought a resounding end to the Ross hoax, but their story is interesting too for what it did not reveal. It said nothing about Folkes's claim, in a letter to the Prime Minister dated 4 April 1942 (printed in full on page 33), that he had known for some time about enemy agents hiding in Rotorua and was keeping a close eye on them . . . and nothing about his further claim of 10 June that the number of miscreants had swelled to 24, who might soon be reinforced by even more invaders of their kind delivered from German or Japanese ships, to spread mayhem that could be beyond the capacity of the Security Intelligence Bureau to check unless it was given much wider powers, including the power to arrest and imprison without going through the tedious business of proving guilt in a court of law. And *Truth* readers read very little about the mountain of misinformation that had been passed to the Security Intelligence Bureau by Ross, to be embroidered and added to by Folkes, and then passed on to the Prime Minister.

These neglected delinquencies have been missing from the oft-repeated handful of anecdotes that are all that have been known of the story ever since, so that Folkes has always appeared as a gullible fool rather than a busy miscreant.

With Ross exposed as a successful super-hoaxer, attention had to focus on the butt of his antics: Major Folkes.

On the day following the explosive issue of *Truth* the Acting Prime Minister, Hon. D.G. Sullivan,took charge:

Major Folkes,
Director of the Security Bureau,
Wellington

Dear Major Folkes
    In view of the recent publication in 'Truth' of an article alleging that the Department of which you are the head has been hoaxed by one 'Captain Calder', a convicted criminal, and in view also of the fact that attempts will doubtless be made to give further publicity to the matter, which publicity might, in view of the nature of the topics involved (such as reference to vital points etc.) be most harmful or prejudicial to the public safety, it is essential that no possibility of any leakage regarding the subject matter or the activities of your department in connection therewith should be allowed to exist.
    Will you, therefore, please at once arrange for the handing over to the Commissioner of Police for delivery to me of all books and documents, photographs, films and

papers of every kind whatsoever including notes and drafts relating to this matter.

I regard immediate compliance with this direction as being of the first importance.

Yours sincerely,
D. G. Sullivan
Acting Prime Minister

In his reply Folkes diverted as much blame as he could onto his deputy, Captain Meikle in Auckland.

Honourable D.G. Sullivan, M.P.,
Acting Prime Minister,

Dear Mr. Sullivan,
Thank you for your letter of the 30th instant which Superintendent [Cummings] handed to me when he called at my office.

It so happens that I conveyed this information to Mr. Cummings, that I have not, at this Headquarters, any documents or articles of any description relating to the case as the whole of the investigations were dealt with by the Auckland Bureau, and any documents, articles, etc., apart from those already in the hands of the Police are in Auckland. I have telephoned to Auckland this afternoon with instructions for such documents etc., as there are in existence, to be brought down by safe hand immediately and as soon as they are in my hands (tomorrow – Friday) they shall be handed to the police for delivery to you in accordance with your desire.

I would like to see you upon this matter whenever you can find it convenient to see me.

Yours sincerely,   K. Folkes

The papers that streamed to Wellington from the Auckland office of the Security Intelligence Bureau were passed to the Attorney General, Hon. Henry Greathead

Rex Mason, who recommended to the Prime Minister on 11 August 1942 that he should report to Cabinet on the whole matter. In the event the decision that he should report came from the War Cabinet (on the same day). The minute read:

> That the Attorney General enquire and report to War Cabinet upon –
>
> *(1) The Security Department's actions in relation to the matter of the Ross allegations.*
> *(2) Whether those actions raise questions as to the competence of the officers of the said Department or any of them.*
> *(3) Whether the circumstances raise a question as to the expediency of continuing the separate existence of the said Department.*
> *(4) That the Director of the said Department and all its officers furnish to the Attorney-General all information and hand to him all documents called for by him.*

Mr Mason decided to support his reading of the papers that came from Auckland by meeting Major Folkes to seek straight answers from him to some puzzling questions that were raised. For this meeting Mr Mason was joined by the Solicitor General, Mr Cornish, and was aided by a stenographer; and the four of them met in a room at Parliament Buildings on 26 August 1942. To prepare themselves, the two senior lawyers (no doubt with help from officers in their departments) listed 82 questions that should be asked of the Director of Security to get to the bottom of things. These prompts set a very limited agenda that did not press the Major very closely as they explored only the question . . . 'how could you possibly have been fooled by this cheeky jailbird Ross into letting this preposterous situation develop that has now been so humiliatingly revealed to the public?' Following these limited preparations neither the Attorney General nor the Solicitor General ever asked the Director of Security why he had claimed, in letters to the Prime Minister (the first on 4 April), that *he knew about conspirators hiding in Rotorua even before he heard of them from Ross,* and how there could have been even a shadow of truth in that clearly worded claim.

One can imagine the tense interview, with the Major cornered and defensive, while admitting nothing – and ready to gain a little ground by lecturing his listeners on the special nature of security intelligence work in wartime.

The interview opened with an invitation to Folkes to tell how the whole thing started. This he did, beginning with the telephone call to his home from the Prime Minister on 29 March 1942 telling him to come at once to his office. He told how he met the Minister of Public Works and a visitor called Mr Ross, and heard a worrying story about a gang of German invaders who had established themselves and were now in hiding in a central part of the North Island, and then took part in discussions to decide what to do about them. Folkes's telling had some twists in it that will surprise readers of this book: he explained that even before he, Folkes, arrived at the Prime Minister's office, Mr Fraser had decided on Ross's alias of Captain Calder of the Merchant Marine; and that very early in the piece Fraser had decided that the police were to be kept from the case in the meantime (a decision that Folkes presented himself as much at odds with). Major Folkes's telling of the story pictured the Prime Minister as a man heavily burdened by the trials of office and weighed on by events, who was thoroughly taken in by Ross – so that important decisions got off on the wrong foot from the start.

The interrogation then took a predictable course, circling around the differences between straightforward police questioning of suspected persons (which would have exposed Ross's game in five minutes) and the less direct ways of the Security Intelligence officers, who generally left things to their trusted and trained man on the spot to present himself as a friend and confidant of possible enemy agents – so that Ross must not let them know that they were under suspicion . . . because if they suspected that they were they might have done something unexpected or violent – or (worse!) slipped underground, to disappear and re-group later. Folkes explained that anyone suspected of being a security risk had to be handled very carefully. He told his listeners that he was all along very suspicious of Ross, though in the meantime he had reluctantly been obliged to follow the Prime Minister's directions to work with him.

The discussion between Folkes and his interrogators was surprisingly courteous, but in a handwritten note some months later (AG to PM 6 Feb. 1943, Document 3) Mr Mason gave a frank opinion of the Major: '. . . the meanly selfish spirit of dishonesty disclosed in a disposition I observe to seek the credit for subordinates work when things went well and transfer the blame to them if things turned out ill . . .'

Three short clips from the record of the interview will give the flavour of it, with Folkes busy re-inventing his role over the past few months to appear a respectful but critical supporter of the Prime Minister ('I said to the PM, Well, look here . . .'), longing to bring the police and the Chiefs of Staff into his confidence to help with the Ross case; and all with no thought of taking more powers to himself.

(1) *Page 12* 'Always I had it in mind that it [Ross's story] could be a fabrication, and as I said to the Prime Minister and to Mr Semple, we had no corroboration of what Ross said recorded between him and other men. For that reason

of course it could be a complete fabrication. Over and over again I pointed that out to the Prime Minister . . .'

(2) *Page 14* 'I do want to make this plain that I had reached the stage that I said to the Prime Minister 'Well, look here, I should take the police into my confidence in this case . . .' I went to the PM and asked his permission to take the police into my confidence, and I desire to register that because it may be that it has not been brought out, but that is what happened and the spirit of it . . .'

(3) *Page 18*
Att General: '. . . at that time you were practically saying to the PM 'We have not got the powers to take this thing further. If we are going to do that we must have the powers to arrest people.'
Folkes: 'That is quite wrong. That is not my angle at all. The position is this: – I went to the Prime Minister and said "Now may I take the Police into my confidence and the Chief of Staff, because in fact this has gone on far enough". Then I discussed with him powers similar to 18(b) regulations. That is not the power for me to do anything, but powers for the Government as a Government to hold and detain people, and the PM said "yes".'

A little over three weeks later (18 September 1942) the Attorney General delivered his report in the shape of a Memorandum to War Cabinet – the paper that Professor Wood saw when he wrote *The New Zealand People at War* and that is touched upon in the Introduction to this book. It is a crisply written paper of five foolscap typed pages that sums up the Ross case neatly, although it does not penetrate the complicated and much more ambitious game that Folkes was playing. Readers will find a copy of the whole report, as Document 2, on page 132.

CHAPTER 10

BUT COULD AXIS FORCES HAVE LANDED?

Some readers of this book may be thinking that the tale they have read about Syd Ross's great hoax, based on the story that some enemy agents landed in New Zealand in the early years of World War II and joined up with some disaffected Kiwis, was too far-fetched to hold water. Surely the scenario is over the top, because any Axis invaders would have been brought here by submarine, and subs of those days didn't have the range to get all the way from Germany to New Zealand, deposit their passengers on a lonely stretch of coast, and then slink all the way back to Kiel or Wilhelmshaven. Wouldn't the Prime Minister have known (or easily found out) that it was impossible, so that the story could not be true?

Well, as it happens, it would have been quite possible to land Axis agents in New Zealand in 1942, for both the German and Japanese navies had subs that had the range to reach right around the world and the capacity to carry a few extra passengers. As well as submarines, several German surface raiders regularly searched and patrolled the South Pacific oceans to find and sink allied merchant ships. These raiders, sometimes disguised as neutrals or allied ships, are the subject of *German Raiders in the Pacific* by S.D. Waters, a slim cardbound volume in the series *Official History of New Zealand in the Second World War*.

Indeed, several books describe the night-time laying of mines at the approaches to four New Zealand harbours, and either of those two minelayers could easily have landed passengers on secluded beaches if that had been required of them. Late in the war one big 'new model' U-boat (U-862) operated in the Pacific, and its movements have been set out in detail by David Stevens in *U-boat Far From Home* (Allen and Unwin, Australia, 1997). This monster checked the harbour at Napier for worthwhile targets, and spent several evenings lying in Hawke Bay with conning tower exposed, watching through binoculars Napier's citizens strolling on their lighted-up Marine Parade. There is even some evidence (though Steven does not believe it) that some German sailors landed one night and found their way to a dairy farm, and took fresh milk back to U-862. What a luxury fresh milk would have been if you were a U-boat crewman who had made do for months with powdered milk stirred into water that had been sitting for months in a steel tank in the bowels of a U-boat!

But during World War II did the Germans ever deliver agents by surface vessels or submarines to enemy shores? They did indeed, several times, and the account that follows describes a penetration by two agents (Coleplaugh and Gimpel) on the Atlantic coast of the United States near the Canadian border. The text is from *Hitler's Spies* by David Kahn (Hodder and Stoughton, 1978). I have adapted this short passage to remove all references the US to help the reader easily imagine what a similar landing on the New Zealand shore would have been like.

... At about four in the afternoon the big U-boat rose slowly from the ocean bed toward the culmination of its secret mission – to plant German agents in a distant enemy land.

On the darkening surface the wind whipped the sea. Presently the U-boat's master saw through his periscope the sweeping flashes of lighthouses, for, though it was wartime, these continued to operate. Through the gathering dusk they helped him navigate to the wide mouth of a bay – a wide body of deep water that indented to land to a depth of two miles. Moving at only one or two knots the sub moved northwest to reach near the middle of an inner bay and lowered into the muck of the bottom to wait for the early hours of the morning.

It was freezing in the U-boat, for to save electricity the master had kept the heating off. It was silent, too, for the officers and men spoke only when they had orders to give, and then as quietly as possible. But though enemy territory encircled the vessel, an air of confidence pervaded it . . . the crew was tough and well-trained and the master felt secure in his careful preparations.

Inside the U-boat two men bustled about. They shed the sub-mariner's uniforms that they had been wearing for the past few months, and put on civilian clothes. From a satchel they took wads of paper money and divided it equally, and each put a sheaf in his wallet. They checked the contents of the suitcase they shared.

Just after 3 o-clock the U-boat's motors started again and the sub lifted until the glistening conning tower just emerged from the water. Almost submerged, the craft glided toward the shore until it was only 500 yards away – then it stopped and swivelled to face south, ready for a fast getaway. Two crew members clambered out and steadied an inflated rubber boat to which was attached a thin rope for pulling it back, empty, to the sub. They put the suitcase in the boat.

Then the pair emerged, hatless, from the conning tower. They shook hands with the master, and with their friends among the crew, and climbed into the rubber boat . . . the light rope had parted and had to be discarded and two sailors climbed in to row the inflatable back to the U-boat – and now they pulled quietly for the dark coast over the slapping black water. The shore gave no sign of life . . . and soon their little boat scraped on a pebbly beach.

The two agents sprang to shore and received their luggage, and the sailors jumped on shore too so that they could boast that they had invaded an enemy country . . . then they *heiled Hitler*, farewelled the two agents, climbed into the rubber inflatable, and quickly returned to their submarine.

The two agents picked up the luggage, turned their backs to the sea, and began walking up the beach. Soon the pine trees swallowed them up.

The first German surface raider of World War II to penetrate the Pacific was the *Orion*. She left Germany in April 1940 and sailed into hostile waters north of Iceland and then hurried due south, right down the coastal waters the length of North and South America, round Cape Horn and across the Pacific, to arrive in New Zealand waters on 13 June 1940. On board she had 228 contact mines, all to be laid in the approaches to Auckland Harbour. They took seven hours to lay, with the last one dropped at 2.36 in the morning (astonishingly, two warships – HMNZS *Achilles* and HMS *Hector* – arrived at Auckland while minelaying was going on, but the *Orion* was not spotted). The German ship sailed off into the Pacific, and the mines she had laid started to sink ships – the first was the *Niagara* (13,415 tons) inward-bound from Vancouver.

From July to mid-August the *Orion* sailed the Tasman and could easily have landed hostile agents on a New Zealand coast if that had been required of her. She then sailed from these waters, and by chance met the *Turakina* (9,691 tons) under Captain J.B. Baird. The captain got off a radio message, turned the stern of his ship to the *Orion*, and opened up with his 4.7-inch gun. There followed the first sea battle ever fought in the Tasman Sea. After an hour the unarmoured and lightly armed *Turakina* was sunk, and the *Orion* had rescued twenty survivors.

The next surface raider to sail from Germany to New Zealand was the *Komet* (Captain Eyssen), which reached the Pacific in August 1940 after an astonishing voyage from Germany, round Norway and through the narrow strait (*Matochkin Shar*) that divides the long Russian island Novaya Zemlaya, whose shape looks rather like an ill-drawn upside down and back-to-front New Zealand, and then with the help of a Russian ice-breaker (Germany and Russia were not yet at war) east across the Arctic Ocean far to the north of Siberia, past Wrangel Island and down through the Bering Strait that divides Russia from Alaska, past the string of Aleutian Islands, and into the Pacific.

In October 1940 the *Komet* joined the *Orion* and the supply ship *Kulmerland* (from then neutral Kobe – Japan had not yet entered the war) to make trouble for allied shipping in the Pacific.

On 25 November 1940 the *Komet* captured and sank the *Holmwood* (564 tons) that was steaming from the Chatham Islands to Christchurch, and, soon after, the passenger liner *Rangitane* (16,712 tons) was spotted. Her master, Captain Upton, turned her stern to the *Orion* and increased to full speed but was soon sunk, although all surviving crew and passengers were rescued and after a month at sea released on Emirau Island.

Next, the small German raider *Adjutant* (350 tons), that looked like a harmless minesweeper, but was in fact a minelayer whose job was to lay ten mines across the entrances of Lyttelton and Wellington Harbours. The mines were laid all right, but every single one was defective and none ever went off. (It seems that in the early years of the war the German navy was ill-served by explosive devices, for when in July 1941 the *Orion* fired the astonishing total of ten torpedoes to sink the British tramp steamer *Chauser,* none detonated.)

The next chance for an Axis ship to land agents on New Zealand shores could have been late in 1941 when the huge Japanese sub I-25 patrolled our coast. This monster was 108 metres long and displaced 2,600 tons, with a top surface speed of 23.5 knots. I-25 was already a veteran of Pearl Harbor and the US west coast, and was big enough to carry a small seaplane that could be disassembled and stowed away inside when the ship submerged. In March 1942 (just about the time Syd Ross was preparing to leave Waikeria prison to start his escapade), the little seaplane carrying a pilot and an observer flew over Wellington and a few days later Auckland Harbour to look for Allied ships – it found too few to bother about, but neither was the plane spotted and identified. The big submarine then folded and reloaded its portable seaplane and sailed off up the east coast of the North Island, where it could have landed enemy agents.

As it turned out, I-25 had an eventful but unproductive visit to New Zealand. It slipped between New Zealand and Australia and came across the trans-Tasman ferry *Monowai,* which it attacked with a torpedo that exploded prematurely. I-25 surfaced to finish off the *Monowai,* to find that the ferry was not the helpless civilian victim it expected, but had been prepared for just such a peril by being converted to an armed merchant cruiser armed with 6-inch guns that were delivering a hail of shells in its direction. The sub submerged quickly and neither ship suffered damage.

Then there was the big German U-boat that we have already noticed early in this chapter: U-862, whose long voyage is so carefully described by David Stevens in *U-boat Far From Home.* Late in 1944 the German High Command accepted that U-boats had been defeated in the Atlantic, and looked for more distant areas where Allied naval defences against submarines would be weaker and sinkings of merchant ships easier to bring off. U-862 was a big new submarine of conventional design, but very well equipped with radar, electronic hydrophones with range and direction finders and all sorts of advanced equipment. An ingenious device was a small autogyro that folded away for storage . . . when needed it was unpacked and assembled, then mounted by the pilot, while the surfaced U-boat faced into the wind and increased speed until the rotor blades on the autogyro turned at about 350 rpm, causing the motorless device to rise while tethered to the sub (so that it could be pulled back down and recovered). When airborne the pilot could look around with binoculars and report to the conning tower by telephone what he saw from his high viewing platform which extended the U-boat's horizon by about 40 km. The portable unpowered autogyro was useful for spotting distant ships, but would have been a pest if hostile aircraft turned up and the sub had to dive suddenly. (I am bound to say that I have doubts about the way the machine is described as getting lift, but this is the only account of it that I can find.)

In a swell the outfit must have looked extraordinary, as the hostile German observer crouched on his platform rising and falling with the troughs and crests of the waves while tethered and pulled forward by a sinister dark vehicle in the sea below.

U-862 (Captain Heinrich Timm) was sent to the Pacific Ocean to work the east coast of New Zealand, crossing the Tasman and passing North Cape on 7 January 1945 and Poverty Bay on 15 January.

> . . . during the day you can see people walking down the street. A man makes a fire on the beach. At dusk we are outside Gisborne harbour entrance . . . went into the harbour. The docks are brightly illuminated, behind them a large factory. You can see cars with their headlights driving along the streets. The street lighting itself is very bright, we are blinded by it. The houses are all brightly illuminated, it looks like Christmas. Our hopes however were not fulfilled, there are no worthwhile steamships at anchor in the dock

for us to sink. Yes, the people here are all so wonderfully unsuspecting. Reversed course . . . carefully we creep out of the harbour . . .

Next day Timm ordered his U-boat into Hawke Bay to look at the coaling pier, and that night moved on to Napier, where

There is no darkening anywhere. You can see the street cafes illuminated with bright red lights, couples move to the old tunes played by the dance music. The town lies on a hill and glitters with a thousand lights . . .

The sailors looked in astonishment at the sight of a town at peace, and the breeze brought the sound of music. With these close contacts in mind, fanciful stories about German invaders don't seem too unlikely after all.

The U-boat then sailed for Wellington, but while going down the Wairarapa coast Captain Timm received a radio message ordering him to leave New Zealand waters and return immediately to his base in Jakarta. He went on past Cook Strait and the east coast of the South Island and rounded Stewart Island to leave New Zealand – into the Tasman Sea on 21 January 1945.

Axis naval forces visited New Zealand waters several times during World War II, so that the story that enemy agents were landed here was quite plausible – it could have happened. Add to that the strenuous radio surveillance of U-boats in the Atlantic from receiving stations round New Zealand, and the regular shipment of troops, aircrew and food to allies on the other side of the world, and close support for allies battling the spread of Japanese forces in the Pacific, and we know that New Zealand was a closely engaged partner in the struggle against the Fascist enemy powers.

CHAPTER 11

MAJOR FOLKES FACES THE MUSIC

Organization For National Security
Chief of Staffs' Committee

C.O.S. paper No. 156:
SECURITY INTELLIGENCE BUREAU
22 December, 1942

1. We have considered a suggestion which has
been advanced that arrangements should be
made for tests to be conducted by the Security
Intelligence Bureau of the effectiveness of
the security precautions to places to which
access is controlled by Naval, Military or
Air personnel or the Police Department. In
discussing this proposal we have found it
necessary to have regard to the present control
of this organization and the fact that it has
recently been the subject of an enquiry by the
Hon. the Attorney General.

2. The Director of the Security Intelligence
Bureau is Major K. Folkes, an Imperial officer
who was seconded for service in New Zealand
to control this organization. We are satisfied
that Major Folkes is not fitted to control the
Security Bureau. Some months ago he approached
us and asked that a number of soldiers be
placed under his orders to assist in the arrest
of certain persons who were alleged to be
Fifth Columnists and about to engage in a huge
sabotage plot which was to synchronise with an
attempted invasion of New Zealand at or near
the port of New Plymouth.

3. In the course of the discussion it transpired that Major Folkes had been in possession of knowledge of the alleged invasion attempt for some months, but notwithstanding this he had never, as he should have done, advised the Chiefs of Staff who are responsible for the defence of the Dominion. The inherent improbabilities and indeed the ridiculous nature of the alleged invasion attempt were quite patent to us at the time but we cannot emphasise too strongly that it is the **duty** of any person who possesses information of this kind to communicate it to those who are responsible for the defence of [one typed line of text is indecipherable] . . . Major Folkes was most definite that it was true and that it was necessary to arrest and detain the conspirators.

4. In the event this invasion and sabotage plot proved to be nothing more than a gigantic hoax and what little we know of the incident gives very strong reasons for believing that the leaders of the Security Intelligence Bureau were negligent and indeed distinctly incapable.

5. In all the circumstances we strongly recommend that the services of Major Folkes should be immediately dispensed with and that he should be returned to the United Kingdom.

6. We are not at this juncture in a position to say whether or not the whole organization should be disbanded. Before furnishing our views on this question we would wish to discuss the position with the Commissioner of Police. The Security Intelligence Bureau has been of value in testing and providing security precautions particularly in connection with shipping and wharves. A certain amount of duplication does exist but with proper organization this can be eliminated.

Signed by <u>E Puttick</u> (Lieut-General)
Chief of General Staff

<u>R.V. Goddard</u> (Air Commodore)
Chief of Air Staff

<u>Atwell Lake</u> (Commodore)
Chief of Naval Staff

From Major Kenneth Folkes
Director of the New Zealand Security Intelligence Bureau

To The Prime Minister
Rt Hon P Fraser, P.C.   17th February, 1943

Sir,
    I beg to thank you for the sight of the
Chiefs of Staff paper No. 156 and desire to
make the following observations.
    The recommendations of the Chiefs of Staff
are manifestly made upon and following the
Report of the Hon. Minister of Justice on
the Ross case. As you know I have already
addressed myself to you in writing concerning
that report, which, as I averred, is based on
insufficient knowledge. It follows therefore
that the present recommendations of the Chiefs
of Staff are grossly unjust, for, in terms
of their own Memorandum, they refer to 'what
little they know of the incident' (para 4) — a
fact which is exemplified by their complaint
'that they were not told about the invasion
for some months . . .'' obviously they are not
aware of the important fact, namely, that you
as Prime Minister were in full possession of
the relevant facts and that your permission
was sought and obtained to inform the Chiefs
of Staff of the same.
    At the end of the paper appears a beggardly
compliment to this organization for work in
connection with security tests. I am bound to

point out that such work does not represent 1% of its activities. May I say with every possible emphasis that only those who see the whole of the work of the organization **from within** are competent to assess its scope and value. Not a single official of any kind — Ministerial or Military — has yet done this, nor does it appear understood that the Organisation is the accredited Representative in New Zealand of the Empire Security Service.

The Paper from the Chiefs of Staff palpably shows that because of the Ross case they have no confidence in me. Unless therefore their views are corrected, I must ask to be released from my present position immediately, and if the stigma against my military reputation contained in the paper from the Chiefs of Staff is to be recorded, then I say that it is unwarranted and I cannot accept it, and I would seek an enquiry, to which, under military law, I am entitled.

The action of the Chiefs of Staff in passing censure without affording me an interview with them, is only typical of the treatment that I have received at the hands of certain officers at Army Headquarters, and also at the Police Headquarters, and against which I have protested most strongly. Upon all these matters I have from time to time written to the Hon. Minister of Defence and others, but I failed to obtain any action or redress or even acknowledgement of the receipt of my correspondence.

Pending your consideration of paragraph 4 of this letter I would be glad to have leave of absence which I find absolutely essential for reasons of dignity and health.

May I have your permission, if you please, at once?

I have the honour to be, Sir,
    Yours obediently

[Signed]   Kenneth Folkes
           Director Security Intelligence

From The Prime Minister
To Major K Folkes   19th February, 1943

Sir,

I have to acknowledge receipt of your letter
of the 17th February and I have carefully
noted the observations you have made. In the
circumstances I think it is best to accede to
your request that you should be released from
your present position and you are accordingly
released as from today.

   The Government will pay the cost of your
return to the United Kingdom and I shall ask
the Secretary of the Treasury to discuss with
you any further details as to salary, leave,
etc., that may arise.

   I shall be grateful if you will at once
hand over the control of your organization,
including all records, to Superintendent
Cummings of the Police.

                         Yours faithfully,
                         P. Fraser
                         Prime Minister

Poor Major Folkes! His request for leave of absence
has been conveniently responded to as though it was a
resignation – and then that resignation is immediately
acceded to, without any of the softening courtesies that a
senior officer might expect on his departure.

What are we to make of him? Remember that he was
appointed head of the New Zealand Security Intelligence
Bureau in 1941, and left Great Britain as Lieutenant
Folkes, but was promoted in transit and arrived here as
Major Folkes. His sudden advance in rank must have
been hard to adjust to, and so must have been entry
into a colonial society that was very different from the
stratified and more formal one that he knew, and into a
senior job that did not easily gather a circle of friends and

acquaintances. He needed tact and good humour, but was not a thoughtful, imaginative man who could adapt easily to new situations, so took on a brusque formal manner to deal with contacts that for most men are governed by that myriad of informalities and understandings that fellow countrymen share.

As Director of Security he was under the Prime Minister, and there he was uncomfortable because Peter Fraser's Scottish working-class childhood was so different from his own, and anyway their contacts were occasional and fleeting. Folkes seems to have made up his mind to show by example how a man of authority looked and sounded. Ross's worrying story of hidden enemies loose in New Zealand gave him the chance to show how things should be done.

When the *Truth* exposure knocked him flat on his face, Folkes put a new spin on events. When interviewed by the Attorney General (see pages 101–2), he tried to reinvent his role in the whole affair. The Attorney General was not impressed.

Before World War II Kenneth Folkes Esq. had worked in the office of a carpet manufacturer in the English Midlands. He corresponded with carpet importers all over the world, including the general New Zealand wholesalers Bing Harris and Company of Wellington, one of whose principals was Jack Harris (later Sir Jack).

When Folkes was appointed to be the head of the New Zealand SIB he was surprised to find that one of the officers under his command was his old correspondent Jack. For the following year or two he was a regular visitor to the comfortable Lower Hutt home of the Harrises.

When the war was over, Jack returned to his importing business and set about re-establishing his web of links with overseas firms. To his surprise, Kenneth Folkes duly appeared again in his old occupation in the same carpet-making business that he had worked for before the war, and their correspondence picked up again without a word about all the events in between. Jack Harris, a sensitive and courteous man, told me that if his friend Kenneth chose not to touch on those embarrassing happenings, he would not either, so their letters were confined to day-to-day matters about sorts of carpets and details about shipping them from Britain to New Zealand. In the late 1950s correspondence tailed off as New Zealand started making its own carpets, and imports from the British Midlands declined.

The final sighting I have of Folkes comprises a report by a journalist who used the pen-name 'Corporal' in the issue of 13 November 1946 of the *New Zealand Observer*. It reports a remarkably sympathetic interview with Major Kenneth Folkes at his London club, and presents him as an exemplary officer who had suffered wrongs and unspeakable assaults on his reputation from many places in New Zealand – including the Prime Minister in parliament.

No doubt 'Corporal' had in mind a piece in Wellington's *Evening Post* (16.9.44, page 5) that reported the Prime Minister explaining to Parliament the day before about the organisation called the Security Intelligence Bureau which was set up in New Zealand at the request of the British government to cooperate with intelligence branches all over the Empire. The paper reported Mr Fraser going on to explain that 'the officer sent out from Britain originally to conduct this organization was a grave misfit who was imposed upon by a criminal. It was one of the most extraordinary stories, worthy of Jules Verne'. . . 'I hope the whole story will be written up,' added Mr Fraser. 'It is one of the most extraordinary instances of human credulity I have ever heard of in my life.'

As it happens, these remarks by the Prime Minister are not to be found in Hansard (*NZPD*, Volume 266, page 376, 15 September 1944), reminding us that MPs have some freedom to edit the proofs of their entries before they are published. In this case it seems that some of the Prime Minister's remarks, including his description of his head of security as a 'grave misfit', were deleted from the proofs of the official record, although they were heard and written down by an alert newspaper reporter, to be published next day in Wellington's evening newspaper.

'Corporal' predicted that Folkes would soon write his own account of these misunderstood events and set the record straight, to land the blame for the Ross hoax where it belonged. No such forecast explanation seems ever to have been published.

The journalistic piece put a strong spin on events – to disparage the Prime Minister and the Minister of Public Works, by an editor who clearly had little sympathy with New Zealand's wartime Labour government. 'Corporal''s account of the Folkes affair is thoroughly at odds with the chain of events that I have set out in these pages, and I have copied it in full as Document 5 at the end of this book. Its chief value, if it is truly a report of a meeting in London (and not a New Zealand editor's invention), must be that it gives a sighting of Folkes about a year after World War II ended. It is illustrated with a photograph of the Major with Captain Cutfield of the Wellington office of the Security Intelligence Bureau – which therefore must have been taken after his arrival in New Zealand in November 1940.

To end this account of the *Ross hoax/Folkes affair* we have three glimpses of Syd Ross. The first is from his handwritten letters to the Police Commissioner (July – October 1942). The second is a newspaper report, dated October 1943, of his appearance in the Christchurch magistrate's court (Document 4); and the third is his obituary printed in *New Zealand Truth* on 8 November, 1946 (Document 6).

When Syd Ross confessed to Commissioner Cummings

SECRET SERVICE

REFERENCE IN HOUSE

EARLY OPERATIONS

"What's this secret service we have been hearing about which made inquiries into the motor sales?" asked Mr. A. J. Murdoch (National, Marsden) when the Prime Minister was answering questions connected with the Public Service Commissioner's Estimates in the House of Representatives yesterday afternoon.

Mr. Fraser replied that it was an organisation known as Security Intelligence, which was set up at the request of the British Government to co-operate with Security Intelligence branches all over the Empire.

The officer in charge at present was one of the ablest in New Zealand, Superintendent Cummings, who had been a most successful detective, and who would eventually be Commissioner of Police.

The officer sent out from Britain originally to conduct this organisation was, said the Prime Minister, a grave misfit who was imposed upon by a criminal. It was one of the most extraordinary stories, worthy of Jules Verne, and when it came to his knowledge he told Superintendent Cummings to clear things up, and that was done in twenty-four hours.

"I hope the whole story will be written up," added Mr. Fraser. "It is one of the most extraordinary instances of human credulity I have ever heard of in my life." Members had criticised the organisation under its original control, but what they said about it was not comparable to his own comments.

The *Evening Post* story of 16 September 1944, with remarks of the Prime Minister not to be found in Hansard.

that there was not a scrap of validity in his hoax story, he repeated what he had already said over and over again: that only about a third of the entries about sightings of Axis agents in the Volumes that were the SIB's record of the case had come from him, *so that two thirds had somehow been added by other hands.*

Cummings agreed: he had read through the five Volumes and saw for himself that most of the reported sightings must have been invented by the Security Intelligence Bureau – as he told the Prime Minister:

> *On Tuesday 7 July . . . I told the Rt Hon Prime Minister that I did not believe the story in the books, and I doubted that it was Ross's story . . .*

Ross would have been glad to get this corroboration, as the last thing he wanted was to be blamed for the whole fraudulent mass of misinformation about innocent citizens. Serious inventions on that scale might have got him into *real trouble.* His relief shines through in a note he wrote to Cummings on 21 July:

> *. . . thanking you once again for the decent manner in which you have treated me throughout this business. Yours faithfully, S. G. Ross*

A month later, no doubt with Cummings's help, Syd Ross became a private in the New Zealand Army, working as a baker in the HQ mess at Burnham Camp, near Christchurch. He wrote to thank Cummings, and in further chatty notes asked questions such as 'Have you heard anything of our mutual friends Meikle and Co?' Clearly he was enjoying his new role as a reformed crim, on close terms with the Commissioner of Police. He was 'in the pink'.

Alas, for all these good intentions, Ross offended

c/o Union Jack Club
Christchurch.

Mr Cummings.

Dear Sir,

I line or two to let you know that I am still keeping in the pink. I am established down here as the baker & pastrycook at the Headquarters Mess Burnham. My job consists of knocking up some special bread, and small goods etc. As I am about the first tradesman they have had here they are all very pleased with my stuff.

I don't know if you will get a laugh out of this, (but hope you don't) I have quite a different outlook on things since being here & can assure you that I am going to take every advantage of the chance you have given me.

If at any time I can do anything for you, you know where I am.

Hoping to hear from you soon

All the Best

S.G. Ross.

A letter from Syd Ross to Commissioner Cummings,
8 September 1942

again in less than a year. And was imprisoned again. Ross escaped from Paparoa prison in September 1943, stealing a bicycle to aid his getaway, but soon gave himself up. He was duly found guilty of the bicycle theft. Before the judge passed sentence, he asked Ross whether he had anything to say. Syd Ross, the natural performer, grasped the moment and let fly with a colourful and highly charged account of his life with the SIB over about five months in 1942. The startled judge and the court newspaper reporters heard (according to the news items that appeared in various newspapers over the following few days) a confusing discourse that clearly did not do justice to the real events that it described. The address certainly did not amuse or impress the unsympathetic judge, who told Ross that he deserved the alias Baron Münchausen for his ridiculous inventions . . . and then asked him why he had escaped from prison, despite the fact that a good part of the address he had just listened to was an explanation of just that.

Poor Ross managed only a lame response: 'Why I told you', surely a dispiriting end to the final public appearance of the man acknowledged to be New Zealand's most ambitious and dramatic hoaxer.

A newspaper report of this court appearance was published in the 8 October 1943 issue of Wellington's *Evening Post*. It appears in this book as Document 4.

The whole story came to an end about three years later, when Sydney Ross contracted tuberculosis and was sent to a hospital in Auckland, where he died on 6 November 1946. His obituary is copied from the *New Zealand Truth* issue of 8 November as Document 6.

New Zealanders have been unlucky to lose sight of Syd Ross and his story. Any man who launches himself on an adventure of the scale he planned, and recruits an unwitting supporting cast that includes the Prime

Minister, the Minister for National Service (Hon. Mr Semple) and the Director of Security deserves to be remembered as a larger-than-life figure. It is a loss for all of us that his brilliant hoax, which was so well known for a while and sparked a creditable television film, has simply faded from memory.

I think Ross's story dipped from public memory because he died so soon after the war, and the security authorities – first the SIB, and then the Special Branch of the New Zealand police, and since 1956 the SIS – simply packed away in files stamped *SECRET* all the interesting details that could have added the story to the public record. No doubt they saw no merit in spreading news of a cornucopia of tales that clearly show the Security Intelligence Bureau to have been a nest of gullible idiots . . . worse – a service whose head had strange ambitions to arrange wide civil powers for himself and some of his officers, and who, to get those powers, conjured up out of thin air the 'evidence' he needed.

The Ross/Folkes story reminds us of the uneasy balance in democratic countries around the world, where secret services that are linked with worldwide networks such as America's CIA and Britain's MI6 coexist with civil governments controlled by elected representatives.

Security intelligence brings a lot of power to its officers that can easily be used to frustrate outsiders by declarations that all sorts of innocent matters (some going back many decades) must be kept secret to preserve the security of the state. We are fortunate that the papers that the present Ross/Folkes story is based on were not so withheld, and were passed to a persistent researcher with little delay or difficulty.

The *Ross hoax/Folkes affair* of 1942–43 is a beautifully clear example of misuse of power by a secret service organisation. In this case Major Folkes, Director of the SIB, used a simple existing hoax, by conman Syd Ross, a hoax that was running its course, to fuel his own much bigger and more elaborate plans. Suddenly Ross's supposed band of four or five invaders was turned into a troop of twenty or so that was expected soon to expand by secret landings from enemy ships, and by local recruitment, into a menacing host bent on sabotage and assassination, and that could be subdued by New Zealand's defensive and police forces only if the government gave him, Major Folkes, and his Security Intelligence Bureau, wide new powers (outside regular legal procedures and based on regulations in force in Great Britain when German invasion threatened in 1939) to deal with the matter.

Folkes seems to have had in mind arbitrary arrest and detention – and goodness knows what further penalties – all at his command ... presumably to be applied to New Zealand residents whom he judged to be imperfectly committed to the Allied cause. It is very hard to imagine what would have happened if the government had panicked and acceded to the urgent demands of its Director of Security and enacted 18(b)-type regulations, and passed the administration of them to a (necessarily greatly expanded) Security Intelligence Bureau.

As that Bureau got into its stride the first citizens to be detained would, no doubt, have been those listed in the five big volumes that we have read so much about, and that we know to be filled with fraudulent entries. What a mass of fusses and anxieties would have been occasioned, with such indignities and injustices caused. The idea does not bear thinking about ... and what a sour end it would have been to Syd Ross's and Charlie Remmers's cheeky hoax, born amid gusts of laughter and merry anticipation in Waikeria prison just a few months before.

DOCUMENTS

Report by Police Commissioner

NEW ZEALAND POLICE DEPARTMENT

WELLINGTON, C.1.
9th August, 1942

MEMORANDUM *for*

The Right Hon Prime Minister,
WELLINGTON

[Handwritten note by the Prime Minister: Referred to Attorney General P.F.]

I forward herewith reports showing the results of Police inquiries into the allegations as to an invasion of New Zealand by certain Germans who, it was stated, were to arrive in a submarine at Otaki on the 11th July last with practically £1,000,000 to assist fifth columnists already working secretly in New Zealand and who were to be ready to assist the Japanese Navy and Army on their arrival at New Plymouth on the 2nd August.

After reading the first of the five volumes constituting the file prepared by the Security Intelligence Department it was obvious that the whole thing was a hoax. The further I read the more I became astounded that the Security Intelligence Department should have been so easily deceived by Ross who, from the outset, was known to them as a bad criminal. Fully half a dozen members of the Security Department from the head down were just clay in Ross's hands. He fooled them consistently for practically four months and appears to have had the time of his life touring the North Island contacting mythical fifth columnists. He had a fast touring car – a lavish supply of benzine – plenty of cash supplied by the Security Department – lived at the best hotels and entertained people at the expense of the Department – all on the pretence that he was contacting fifth columnists. The volumes compiled by the Security Department show how lavishly Ross lived and how he was forced to continue in the work he was engaged on. Ross was so urged to action at times that I wonder he did not do some damage to vital points to justify the whole scheme. I was amazed when I heard that Ross was employed by the Security Department and had the means of travelling over the whole North Island in a fast moving car with an unlimited supply of benzine, and would not have been surprised had he damaged Arapuni or some other electrical works as evidence of the correctness of his story as to the proposed activity of fifth columnists. He appeared to have been supplied with data relating to the various vital points in New Zealand.

Ross was not slow to observe that he was dealing with a Department composed of amateur detectives who were unable to see through him. He had some of them chasing him around the North Island in a motor car to observe him make contacts with the alleged fifth columnists. I feel justified in saying that any man who is not capable of seeing through Ross, particularly when conversant with his criminal history, is unfit to be employed on security work. The whole thing was so palpably a hoax that it is difficult to understand why Ross was permitted to carry on for so long and given the means and opportunity of adding to his criminal record. Surveillance over him by the Security Department was deplorably absent.

When the inquiry was handed over to the Department the fact that the whole story was a hoax was laid bare after 1½ days inquiry at Rotorua. Ross, when interviewed by experienced Police Officers, admitted that the whole thing was a hoax. A bad feature of it all was that innocent people, whose names were mentioned as fifth columnists, had to be interviewed in other parts of the North Island simultaneously with the interviewing of Ross in Rotorua. These people were tactfully approached.

I can understand Ross desiring the scheme to be kept secret from the Police as he well knew he could not deceive them. He has been talking for years about some 'jelly' being put into the works at Arapuni.

Had Major Folkes consulted me in the matter I could have saved him and his senior officers the indignity of being made such fools of by a criminal like Ross who was far too artful and clever for them.

One of the closing scenes in the whole farce was the alleged flogging and proposed death and burial of Ross in Mamaku Bush. It is almost unbelievable, yet facts have established that Ross got a rope clothes line, wet it and pulled it over his bare body to make it appear that he was flogged and tied up while the alleged Germans dug a grave in the bush in which to bury him. Ross brought a spade and dug the grave himself. Ross alleges that he escaped, wandered to a house occupied by a family named Dahlin where he gave a note to Gustav Dahlin for delivery to the Security Department at Rotorua. He gave Dahlin £1 for a taxi to take him to Rotorua although he had only a £5 note left he gave this to Dahlin in case the taxi fare might be more than the £1. Dahlin was to bring back the change. Dahlin, who has just returned from service overseas, put one over Ross as he went to Hamilton for a holiday on the £6 and returned home when the money was spent. He did not deliver the note to the Security Officers at Rotorua.

Ross was subsequently removed from Dahlin's by the Security Officers after he had been attended by Dr Cuddy of Rotorua. Ross fooled them to such an extent that he was carried for about three hundred yards to the car and removed to the Security Department's house at Rotorua where he was waited upon by Security Officers who obviously did not then see through his foolery.

Among other fantastic accounts related by Ross is that of the taking of soundings at New Plymouth on the night of the 4th July and set out at page 595 of Volume 5. It should be remembered that prior to this date New Plymouth had been fixed as the landing place for the enemy forces yet the Security Organisation were prepared to believe that these forces were depending on soundings to be taken by Ross and 'Archer' at some future date and which, when carried out, were conducted in such a childish manner as to be incredible. I draw your attention to the photograph of the clothes line rope appearing at page 581 of Volume 5, the rope allegedly used to take soundings for the landing of an enemy force.

Another instance of childlike simplicity of the alleged enemy operations in this country appears in the account of how Ross contacted one of the enemy agents at Taumaranui on the 18th June, vide pages 18 to 186 of Volume 4. There it is suggested that Ross has only to approach a person whom he has never seen before and tell the person he is Captain Calder, whereupon the person allegedly discloses to Ross or Captain Calder what his part is in the fifth column plan.

These descriptions by Ross of the ease of which he was contacting the enemy agents would suggest to any responsible intelligent person that there was something wrong in his story and that the time had arrived to make some effective check-up on him. That was never done, and leaves no other conclusion than that the Security Organisation were incompetent, to say the least, and that their methods would endanger public safety.

In my whole forty years experience as a Police Officer I have never known of such a case as this – to think that a man now qualified as an habitual criminal could pull the wool over the eyes of men who are supposed to be Security Intelligence Officers is beyond comprehension. Had there been any truth or foundation in this plot then the very methods adopted by the Security Organisation in their investigation would have to a very considerable extent resulted in the failure of their efforts. For instance, a very elaborately detailed invasion plan was set out on page 543 of Vol.4, the dates of the invasion being fixed and the projected movements of the enemy indicated. Up till the time that these records were handed over to the Police it does not appear that the Armed Services were apprised of these facts. On Saturday, 11th July, they were shown to the Deputy chiefs of staff at this office and they commented that from an operational point of view the plan was not practicable. Then there is the fact that of the large number of persons who were allegedly members of the enemy organisation no steps were taken to make a full and proper investigation regarding them. There were alleged to be enemy agents who were landed from a submarine but whose identity was never fixed by the Security Organisation who were prepared to believe that these persons actually existed but were known only to Ross.

Had the story told by Ross been true then it would have been a lamentable state of affairs that the Security Organisation should know of these persons through Ross for a period of some months and yet not been in a position to locate them. If the story were true Ross's life may really have been in danger at times, but if anything had happened to him how would the Security Organisation be able to place their hands on these enemy agents when they wanted them. This shows the degree of incompetence, consistent with their handling of the case all the way through.

The Security Organisation has shown a distrust of the

civil Police which could only be detrimental to the public interest. If there was any real reason to believe a fifth column organisation existed then it was the duty of all the authorities, Police, Security and Military to co-operate and to co-ordinate their activities in such a manner that the organisation would have been properly dealt with. I observe, however, that in this case Major Folkes advised Captain Meikle on the 24th June that the revelation of this enemy activity in New Zealand has been received by the Chief of Staff with incredulity, but that the Chief of General Staff had reluctantly agreed to make available military personnel for the final action.

The very nature of the 'final action', would be such that it was essentially Police work yet this Department knew nothing of it. Captain Meikle recorded on that day that it may be better after all to go back to the idea of overcoming the Police attitude and by winning by some means their co-operation. I have no knowledge of what attitude it was that Captain Meikle felt should be overcome. It would have certainly caused a scandal had this organisation been allowed to proceed with the 'rounding up' of people whose innocence has been proved beyond doubt.

D J Cummings

Commissioner of Police

Report by Attorney General

DOMINION OF NEW ZEALAND

Attorney-General's Office

SECRET   WELLINGTON

18th September, 1942

MEMORANDUM

from the Attorney-General

to War Cabinet:

As directed, I have enquired into certain questions arising out of the Ross case.

The papers in the case form a great bulk. In addition to 600 odd pages of Security file there are a mass of Police reports and a final statement by Ross himself in which it is alleged the true explanation is given and which, though it must finally be judged to be the characteristic work of a false pretences artist, nevertheless adds to the labour involved. It would take too long to endeavour to give anything like a complete story of the events, but in the barest outline they are as follows: Ross was released from Waikeria Prison on the 28th March and that same day rang the Hon Mr Semple in Wellington endeavouring to make an appointment. He was told to see Mr Semple the next day and arrived in Wellington accordingly. He gave his story of having been interviewed by a man named Barrett and that this person was a German agent, and that Barrett desired to employ Ross to commit sabotage, having selected Ross for Ross's well-known ability in the handling of gelignite and in breaking and entering. Mr Semple took the man to the Prime Minister who handed him to Major Folkes. Ross explained that he was recently from prison, that though he was a housebreaker he was not a betrayer of the country, that he desired that the Police be not brought into the matter and that he would give every assistance to unravel the plot. Major Folkes sent him to the Auckland Office of the Security Department and Ross was instructed to meet Barrett as arranged or requested by Barrett. Barrett sent Ross to [R.A.K.] Mason, Editor of 'In Print', who sent him to No.9 Boston Terrace, Wellington, where he was to meet the conspirators. Ross reported that he had met conspirators in Wellington but that the arch conspirator, Rimmer or Remmers, was at Ngongotaha, near Rotorua. Ross accordingly went to Ngongotaha and actually did meet this man Remmers or Rimmer, and alleged that he met four other conspirators living in a house in Rotorua.

Ross usually referred to Remmers as 'the master' and never spoke of him except with a respect that was most impressive and might even be called reverential. This admiration was probably as genuine as it was undoubtedly deserved, for Remmers, an old man, is indeed a master artist in the sphere of false pretences, with a record vastly more imposing than Ross's. There is reason to think Ross's plans owed something to Remmers at critical points. The Security Department was unfortunate in meeting this combination of talent.

Captain Meikle, in charge of the Auckland Security Office, then got four officers of the Department from Wellington to come to Rotorua to reside there in the endeavour to make contact with the conspirators. The method was to frequent the Grand Hotel in the expectation that they might be introduced to them by Ross. Ross meantime was staying at the Grand Hotel as Captain Calder of the Merchant Marine, this being to facilitate contact with and discovery of the conspirators. After some weeks Ross produced a list of names of people in different parts of the North Island alleged to have been given him by Remmers, as other conspirators whom Ross was to meet. Captain Meikle accordingly sent Ross round the North Island to interview these people and accompanying him sent Mr Steven of the Auckland Office. Ross and Steven duly made the trip, interviews were made by Ross who furnished reports of the alleged happenings at the interviews. At Rotorua and New Plymouth and perhaps at other places Ross came under the notice of members of the Police force and others who knew him as a convicted criminal with a record, and with some difficulty the Security Department managed to secure that Ross's masquerade as Captain Calder be not interfered with. The story of an invasion plot had at an early stage been added to the sabotage plot. Major Folkes meantime reported to the Government on the seriousness of the story of the plot as to the truth of which he made no doubt, and urged the Government to take power to arrest the alleged conspirators without proof of any charge against them, in default of which power he would not be responsible for the safety of the country. Ross took a number of steps to impress upon Security the desperate nature of the conspirators, amongst these steps being a ridiculous pretended attempt upon his life. At this stage the Police had been brought into the matter and it took them a very short time to expose the falsity of the whole story which had occasioned Security so much trouble, expense and anxiety over so many months.

This account is most inadequate in view of the picturesqueness of the whole story but is all that time and space will now justify, and it is sufficient for the present purpose.

Security Department files are so different from those in other Departments as to make their appearance most striking and appear to justify a story told by Ross to the Police that the files were a form of journalism made with publication in view. This story, however, as all the other of Ross's accusations against the Security Bureau's integrity and the good faith of their officers, I reject utterly. Ross started out early in life as a false pretences artist; and once a false pretences artist always a false pretences artist. I have never known or heard of criminals of that particular type being converted to honest ways. They delight in their skills at deception. They will go to incredible pains to deceive. The file genuinely tells the story as it presented itself to the Security Bureau. However surprising it may appear, it is the fact that over a period of three months scepticism as to the truth of the story progressively vanished. It was succeeded by acceptance of it, and finally a firm belief in it, and this apparently was only brought to an end by the Police enquiries.

When Major Folkes first received his instructions, he got Ross to tell him the story he had told to Mr Semple and the Prime Minister. It agreed with the first version. He instructed Captain Meikle of Auckland to follow the matter up and watch for the appearance of any motive for lying by Ross. Major Folkes knew that Ross was a convicted criminal, and ought, in my opinion, to have ascertained by judicious enquiries what sort of individual he had to deal with. Even if the avenue of Police enquiries was considered to be closed, another through the Justice Department was open. Major Folkes was wrong in being disposed to accept the story merely on the ground of apparent absence of motive for falsehood. Instructions went to Captain Meikle by phone. He knew Ross had convictions for safeblowing, but at no stage knew that Ross had convictions for false pretences. There seems to have been a weakness here. Major Folkes informed me that he regarded the case as an Auckland one, and that he consequently did not personally keep in close touch with the details when once he had handed it over to Captain Meikle. It is, of course, impossible to accept this view.

Had it appeared that trivial matters were at stake it might have been so, but not in so grave a matter. If Major Folkes did not continuously give direction to the enquiries he was gravely culpable, and if he did closely oversee them he was responsible for them. As head of the Department his responsibility is an exceedingly real, not a nominal one. In fact, he was kept continuously informed of the progress of the enquiry, by telephone, by transmission of files, and personal visits to Wellington of Captain Meikle and his officers.

Why did Captain Meikle not make some of the simplest and most obvious enquiries? Why could he not have contrived some perfectly safe way of finding out – e.g. – whether No.9 Boston Terrace, Wellington, contained the band of conspirators alleged to be living there? And what was the difficulty in ascertaining as the fact was, that the occupants of a certain house in Rotorua, alleged to be four desperate enemy alien conspirators, were really three hospital nurses, an elderly Native Department clerk who daily went back and forth to work, and one alien, who had a small business as a dry cleaner? In one case an attempt was made to check up on Ross. It must be admitted that the attempt made was quite a skilful one. A naval rating was installed in the hospital ward in Auckland in which Remmers was laid up. The idea was a good one. The naval rating proved himself an accurate reporter of what he heard and saw. It was bad luck for the Security Department that the result appeared to confirm Ross's story. This probably helped greatly to mislead Captain Meikle. But at the best the check served only to show that Remmers was an able man. The corroboration affected only a small part of Ross's story and only touched the fringe of the conspiracy.

The real reason for the failure of Security was the system on which it worked. It was very conscious of the difference between its methods and those of the Police. It explains that it does not send a man to take a statement, as the Police do. The Security Department observes, tabulates, accumulates reports, and slowly builds up a picture. It does not check, test, and verify (as far as it can) as it goes along. This method appears to me to manifest that extreme fear of disclosing oneself that is appropriate to secret service in a hostile country, but Major Folkes assures me that its use is not so restricted. Clearly the method can accumulate, and in this case did accumulate, much rubbish.

As to the journey made by Ross and Mr Steven, the question suggests itself at every turn – why was no check made? – and Steven's answer is that his instructions were merely to report Ross's actions and story. This is undoubtedly correct. Mr Steven impressed me as a decent, faithful officer, who would wander neither to the right nor to the left. I think I ought to say also that Captain Meikle appeared to me to be intelligent, conscientious, active, and remarkably meticulous. One does not discern in him any quality that causes one to think lightly of his capacity. He was frank in his statements, and I liked his candour and courage in spontaneously accepting responsibility for all actions carried out by his subordinates. His resignation has been submitted, because he understands that it is required, but I am of opinion that it would be discreditable to make him the scapegoat for what has occurred. He was not responsible for not securing that aid from the Police which was essential.

It would be futile to discuss in detail the mass of rubbish the files disclose. The system showed itself utterly incapable of handling the case. Moreover, there is in our security work duplication and lack of co-operation and co-ordination. This is shown especially in relation to the Police Department. Security seems to regard a New Zealand Police officer as the policeman of the English comic paper. This does not make for co-operation. But, apart from this unfortunate attitude of superiority on the part of Intelligence, existing arrangements would still be ill-adapted to secure the end in view, viz., national security. When taking over port duties, Security never came to a clear understanding with the Police Department. The civil security work which it does is entirely covered by the Police, a fact known to those who have to peruse certain Police files. It is hard to know why such a duplication came to be instituted, more especially as this is work that the Police do well and the Security Department with its distinctive methods could never do.

The Security Bureau appears to have begun its operations in ignorance of the fact that a large part of its proposed work was already being done by the Police, or at all events without consideration of this fact and consequential adjustments. These adjustments, which ought to have been made and were not made, are the important matters; and condemnation of individuals is liable to distract attention from them.

The ridiculous aspect of these proceedings must not obscure their essential gravity. Our Security organisation has for three months shown itself incapable of ascertaining the truth of a pretended plot in such manner as to undermine confidence that it could ascertain the truth respecting a real one. Shortly, two confidence men have applied to our Security organisation a test which has shown the need for re-organisation. Further, Major Folkes's recommendation (fortunately rejected by the Prime Minister) that power should be taken to arrest and detain a considerable number of people without proof of wrongdoing by them, reveals a psychology which, however apt it may be for dealing with security problems in other countries and conditions, is not adapted to New Zealand.

Memorandum by Attorney General

Attorney-General's Office
Wellington
6th February 1943

URGENT

MEMO for
Rt Hon Prime Minister [handwritten]

Security Intelligence Bureau

Further to my report herein, I have to recommend:–

1) Some decision should be made in reference to my report. If the bureau is to remain as at present, that should be as a result of a definite decision.

The contents of my report appear to have become known among the staff, who appear to have learned from the head of the bureau that nevertheless no change will be made. The result appears to be some unrest in the staff due to a feeling of uncertainty.

2) An audit officer should instantly take charge of the account books and conduct an audit, without previous warning reaching the head of the bureau.

Sums from time to time transferred from the bureau funds to the head of the bureau for his disbursement on security work without more explanation are so substantial that staff members cannot imagine any work for which they can properly be required. They therefore are full of anxiety as to the matter, having no means of resolving the grave suspicion which they cannot help feeling.

The suspicion is no shock to me. It is consistent with

the meanly selfish spirit of dishonesty disclosed in a disposition I observe to seek the credit for subordinates' work where things went well and transfer the blame to them if things turned out ill. Nevertheless it is necessary to remember that so far there is not more than suspicion and grounds for enquiry.

As the minister in charge of the department the responsibility for action would appear to rest with you personally in respect of this question of accounts.

H.G.R.M.

Evening Post
8 October, 1943

WHY HE ESCAPED

PRISONER'S CLAIMS

―――――

COUNTER TO JAP PLOTS

P.A. CHRISTCHURCH,   October 7 1943.

A strange tale of counter-espionage work and alleged attempts on his life was told by Sydney Gordon Ross, an escapee from Paparua Prison, who appeared before Mr. E. C. Levvey, S.M., in the Magistrate's Court on charges of escaping from Paparua Prison, being an incorrigible rogue in that he escaped from Paparua Prison, and with unlawful conversion of a bicycle valued at £5, the property of John Edward Bennett. The charge of escaping from gaol was withdrawn, and Ross, who pleaded guilty to the other two charges, was sentenced to nine months' imprisonment with hard labour, the sentence to start at the expiration of the sentence he is now serving.

Sub-Inspector Macnamara said that Ross, who was 33 years of age, was at present serving a sentence of two years and a half with hard labour. At 8.30 p.m. on September 30 he escaped from Paparua Prison, and on his way into the city unlawfully converted a bicycle. On the following morning at 2.20 he called at the watchhouse and gave himself up.

'I will tell you why I escaped,' said Ross when asked if he had anything to say. 'The story goes back about 18 months, just after America came into the war. New Zealand had very little equipment in the country, and there was about £500,000 Japanese money distributed throughout New Zealand. I was ill at the time and was offered a position as a Japanese agent, but this got to the right quarters – the New Zealand Secret Service, so-called – and they practically went down on their bended knees asking me to work for them.'

The Magistrate: Are you the man who was living at Rotorua on the best of everything?

Ross: Yes.

The Magistrate: You ask me to swallow this?

'EYE ON THE QUISLINGS.'

'They asked me to take the rank of captain. I could not be any higher as the man in charge was a major,' continued Ross. 'I was given unlimited power and money. The Navy, Air Force, and Army were placed at my disposal. It sounds foolish here, I know, but it is correct. My first job was with the New Zealand quislings, or fifth columnists, as they are called. The first thing I discovered was that I could trust very few of my colleagues, and second, the rather big names in this thing, New Zealand's 'untouchables'. Anyhow, the Japanese suffered one or two reverses, and the 'untouchables' discovered that they would not have to sell out and that they could go back to their old way of living.

'I worked as Captain Calder for four months and a half, and in that time gave as many shocks as I received. When the 'untouchables' realised that they could go back to their normal mode of living, 'Captain Calder' was not wanted and had to be disposed of. Several newspapers said that 'Captain Calder' had robbed the Government of thousands of pounds, and a weekly, I think it was, asked why action had not been taken. Also several members of Parliament asked for information about it, but all they got was a stony silence.'

After saying that he had come to Christchurch and enlisted in the Army as a private, Ross said that an attempt had been made on his life, two bones in his back being broken, necessitating some two months in hospital. 'It is surprising the number of sums of money offered to me to sell information or to keep silent,' said Ross, 'but I refused as I was finished and had enough. Later an exceptionally large sum was offered me, but I also refused to take it. The Department apparently thought I had been offered a larger sum.'

ALLEGES HE WAS SHOT AT

Ross also alleged that some time later shots had again been fired at him in Christchurch and that two bullets had gone through his clothing. 'Shortly afterwards I was arrested in Christchurch on three petty charges. I do not want you to think I am taking a punch at the police,' continued Ross, 'as I am referring to people higher up. I know that I am not doing myself any good, but I say now that each charge was a dirty frame-up, and I repeat that I am not throwing that at the police. If I had not pleaded guilty I would have been charged on another count. Two men were prepared to step forward and give evidence against me, but if they bring up the other charge now it will only go to prove what I am telling you now.'

Ross said he served a term in prison and then received a letter from one of the persons involved in the affair. People were talking, and perhaps he wanted to do a little himself to save his own hide, said Ross, who then told how he had broken away from prison, arriving in Christchurch at 11.15 p.m. in search of the man who had written the letter. 'My search was futile, and I was a very disillusioned man at 2.15 the next morning, as it was raining. Who would believe it anyhow?' he asked. 'You can visualise my state of mind, as it was cold, wet, and raining. I tore the letter up, walked into the police station, and gave myself up. I do not want you to think I am trying to influence you in any way.'

The Magistrate: No; and I think by your remarks that your alias should be Baron Munchausen. Why did you escape from prison?

Ross: Why I told you.

Item from *New Zealand Observer*

New Zealand Observer
13 November 1946

ECHOES OF
'ROSS FRAUD'

Major Kenneth Folkes, Shackled by Military Secrecy in 1944, Unseals His Lips and Replies to Prime Minister Fraser's Bitter Attack on Him in Parliament

By CORPORAL

- On October 11, 1944, the OBSERVER published a lengthy article by 'Spotlight', which dealt with the activities of the Security Intelligence Bureau, referred in some detail to the case of Sidney Gordon Ross in 1942, and clearly indicated that the Bureau and its head (Major Kenneth Folkes) were more sinned against than sinning.

- Ross, it will be remembered, was an impudent criminal who concocted a weird and wonderful story of a plot to land saboteurs in New Zealand by submarine, blow up the Arapuni dam, assassinate Messrs. Fraser and Semple and other spectacular personalities, and, by these and similar acts of violence, reduce the Dominion to panic and its war effort to frustration.

- In the following interview, written exclusively for the OBSERVER by 'Corporal', Major Kenneth Folkes refutes Mr. Fraser's 1944 statement that he was an 'obvious

*misfit who was imposed on by a criminal', and adds
some terse and illuminating comments.*

UNQUESTIONABLY the 'Ross Fraud' caused the New
Zealand Government great political embarrassment
during the hectic days between 1942 and 1944. Both
before, during and after the 'fraud', Major Kenneth Folkes
was the head of the New Zealand Security Intelligence
Bureau. When the 'fraud' was discussed in Parliament
back in 1944, the Prime Minister said of his Security
Chief: 'He was an obvious misfit who was imposed on
by a criminal.'

Would Major Folkes tell the full story? This was the
question I addressed to him when I met him at his London
club the other day.

There were many in New Zealand who felt at the time
that the Prime Minister's public castigation of an Imperial
Army officer behind the shelter of Parliamentary privilege
savoured of the Gestapo methods which, rightly or
wrongly, were associated by the public with the activities
of the Bureau.

In any case, I can now say that Major Folkes keenly
resents the Prime Minister's attack on him. He was
reluctant to give me the intimate details of the great
'fraud'. That is a story for the future. It may be assumed
that the Prime Minister's hope, as expressed by him in
Parliament, that the story of the case would be enshrined
in print, is likely to come to fruition.

If I am not mistaken, the author will be none other
than Kenneth Folkes – and who better could there be
to tell it? When the full story is told, Major Folkes may
not appear to be the 'misfit who was imposed on by a
criminal'. Perhaps, indeed, it will be our worthy Prime
Minister and his henchman Robert Semple who will be
so labelled – if such a description is deserved at all.

A "MISFIT" INDEED!—The redoubtable Major Folkes (right) with one of his former officers, Captain R. S. Cutfield, who later served overseas with the Air Force.

Ministers Involved Knee-deep

BEYOND doubt, Messrs Fraser and Semple were inextricably involved in the case from its beginning to its end.

I gather that Major Folkes's story will be that these two gentlemen expressly instructed Major Folkes that he was not to reveal any details whatsoever of the case to the police or to the Chiefs of Staff.

> **Before the Major ever came into the picture, Ross seems to have gained an Interview with the Prime Minister and Mr. Semple in the former's room early one Sunday morning, and to have so impressed them with his story that they gave him their solemn word that his name would not be disclosed to the police or to the military authorities.**

Messrs. Fraser and Semple knew – for Ross himself told them – that Ross was a criminal and had been released from gaol the day before. The fact that he was an expert with dynamite and a first-class safe-blower (to quote the Prime Minister's own words) was said to be the reason why he had been approached by enemy agents.

Kenneth Folkes says definitely that the Prime Minister himself closed one of the accepted avenues of security inquiry by giving Ross the promise which he did.

This, however, is merely by the way. What happened to Kenneth Folkes after his resignation and departure from New Zealand? He was still an Army officer, and charged with important and serious duties. His military superiors did not question his suitability or ability for important posts.

He was successively engaged on important operations in Balkan and French territory ahead of military occupation, while in Italy he was in command of his own unit of political intelligence under the aegis of the Foreign Office.

After that, he was in Austria, where his work was chiefly concerned with the apprehension and 'screening' of Nazis and war criminals. Perhaps his superiors in the Imperial Army were more impressed by the letter of high commendation which the late Rt. Hon. J. G. Coates (then Minister for War Co-ordination) handed to him when he left New Zealand than by the criticisms with which he was belaboured at the same time.

That he had enemies cannot be gainsaid. Indeed, it would be difficult to believe that anyone in his position could fail to make enemies – if he did his job impartially and fearlessly.

Low Opinion of Mr Fraser!

FOR the people of New Zealand and its armed forces, Kenneth Folkes has the highest regard. He personally observed some of the exploits of the 2nd New Zealand Division in Italy, and the pride of New Zealanders in their soldiers is fully shared by him.

> This is what he says, and the remark is not exactly flattering: 'If some of the political heads in power in the Dominion had anything approaching the stamina and decency of its soldiers, New Zealand would indeed be a paradise.'

Of those political heads, and particularly of the Prime Minister, Major Folkes has a decidedly unflattering opinion. 'How,' he asks, 'could I feel otherwise? Was I not a soldier, detailed for service in New Zealand from no wish or seeking of my own? Was I in New Zealand at the time when the Prime Minister chose to attack me personally, and this in the most public of all places – i.e., Parliament? As an Army officer, could I defend myself? Had I not resigned my appointment and become engaged in service in more active theatres of war? My lips were sealed then, but not now.'

He told me that the Security Intelligence Bureau was established in the Dominion at the request of the New Zealand Government, and that he was the officer detailed by the British War Office to organise and control it.

It was by no means the most pleasant of duties. Intelligence work seldom is – and particularly the security branch. But the conditions which he found in New Zealand convinced him of the wisdom of the decision to implement security measures in accordance with the accepted principles in use in Great Britain and the United States.

Proof of Existing Futility

IN the early stages, Major Folkes's efforts were by no means welcomed by the powers-that-be. There were many in the Army who did not like the Bureau. The police considered that they could do the work quite efficiently (although they hadn't done so!), in spite of the fact that they had not been trained in military security.

Such was the obdurate attitude of the police and others to 'security' that Major Folkes was obliged to prove the necessity for the many security measures which he so earnestly advocated and which were eventually adopted. And surely these contributed to the immunity which New Zealand enjoyed?

The security of the waterfronts passed from the police to the Security Intelligence Bureau only after Major Folkes and his loyal staff had demonstrated that the then existing measures were positively futile.

In order to prove his assertions, did not some of his officers make no fewer than three separate entries to the floating dock (one of them swam to it from the shore) and innumerable entries upon wharves and shipping, walking past the so-called 'guards' without question?

Did not another officer gain entry to a different establishment, take photographs of a gun breach, and then remove the cartridges of the 'guard' without detection? And so on *ad infinitum*? Did not Major Folkes's Dominion-wide 'Don't Talk' campaign have effect? Did not his Bureau run to earth some of the scandals connected with Mr. Semple's National Service Department – for instance, the celebrated ballot scandal?

Leakage About U.S. Forces

THE necessity for the 'Don't Talk' campaign may be illustrated by the story – in brief – of the leakage of the destination of the American Marine force assembled in Wellington Harbour in 1942.

Major Folkes recalled that, some 10 or 11 days before the departure of this force from New Zealand, one of his officers learned that, in a Wellington tramcar, a man was heard to say that the Americans were bound for the Solomons.

According to Major Folkes, the greatest possible secrecy was supposed to have been observed in connection with this operation, and not more than three departmental heads knew at that time what the destination was.

Yet here was the statement, made quite openly in a public tramcar seven days before the scheduled arrival of the naval task force, that the destination was the Solomons!

Within two days of this statement being made the Security Intelligence Bureau had investigated and fixed complete responsibility for the leakage. Not a bad effort on the part of an organisation which had been largely developed and commanded by a 'misfit'!

Just what happened? The husband of a young woman employed by a Government department expressed curiosity to his wife as to the destination of that large fleet of ships in the Wellington Harbour. Did she know where they were going? No, she didn't.

Later, however, something happened in her department which gave her a clue. A large bundle of charts was withdrawn from its accustomed place in the department, and she promptly took energetic steps to find out what they were and who had them.

It did not take much time or mental effort for her to discover that the charts were of the South-west Pacific; and then, later, she ascertained that they were of the Solomons area.

What could be clearer? The Americans were going to the Solomons. She promptly satisfied her husband's curiosity, and next morning in the tramcar, he spilled the beans.

A good guess, you may say. Not so good when all the circumstances are known. It was a very abashed young woman who faced the Security Intelligence chief two days later. The case was never publicised. Like so many others, it just couldn't be.

No, the suggestion that Kenneth Folkes was a 'misfit' doesn't quite ring true.

Not a Gestapo

NOW, the Security Intelligence Bureau had the reputation of being a sort of Gestapo. Was this reputation deserved? Kenneth Folkes says definitely, 'No.' But might it have been, if it had been under less capable direction?

Major Folkes doesn't plead infallibility, by any means. He does not attempt in any way to shelve responsibility that may be his for the Ross case, even though he saw the criminal only once, and that in the Prime Minister's room with Mr. Fraser and Mr. Semple both present.

As chief of the Bureau, he accepts full responsibility for the actions of his departmental officers, as any reasonable superior should and must do. For his own staff he has the highest praise, and keenly resents any reflections cast upon them.

> 'Perhaps,' he says, 'when the truth comes out, it will be seen that there was a lot more in the Ross case than met the eye; and also that it was worth a good deal of the time expended on it in order to reveal the perfidy of a good many persons and the 'ham' methods of a certain blue-uniformed organisation.'

It is significant to recall that Mr. Fraser's attack on Major Folkes was in his (Mr. Fraser's) defence in the political embarrassment in which he found himself. Questions of loyalty to one's subordinates were clearly involved (for the Prime Minister was Folkes's only boss); and in this connection it should be noted that Major Folkes did not shift responsibility to Mr. Fraser, who was as fully aware of the facts of the Ross case as Folkes was.

Major Folkes admits that daily reports of the case were submitted to him; but they also went through to the Prime Minister and to Mr. Semple at their express request.

Long before the exposure of Ross, the Security Intelligence Bureau had its own ideas on the subject. In fact, it was at the direct request of Major Folkes that the case was brought to a head and he was granted permission to inform the chiefs of Staff and the police of the situation.

Nevertheless, caution must always be the keynote of all security work. If subordinates in the Bureau appeared to take a long time to satisfy themselves that Ross (and a few other people) were frauds, that, says Major Folkes, is no justification for a personal attack on an officer (*in absentia*) by the head of the Government (who was aware of everything which was going on) – particularly when that officer, because of his military oath of secrecy, was unable to defend himself without breaking that oath.

Bureau Wouldn't Play Politics

REVERTING, however, to the 'Gestapo' charge: time and again, Major Folkes states, the Bureau was asked to investigate responsible and other citizens whose activities were alleged to be sabotaging the war effort.

> More often than not, they were in no way related to the war effort. In truth, they were mostly flavoured with political colourings or ideologies inimical to the party in power.

As such, the Bureau observed its inflexible rule and left all such complaints severely alone, much to the annoyance of certain members of the Government, and to one in particular.

'In this respect,' commented Major Folkes, 'I could well understand my refusal to deviate from the strict path, causing some people to say I was a misfit!'

At no stage was the Bureau political. It preached and practised the importance of the gospel of security (military and civil) up and down the land. It checked and cross-checked to prevent possible leakage, even from those in high places, but it never interfered specifically with the everyday activities of any one person more than another.

Of course, the activities of the Bureau were not confined merely to leakages of information. Its scope was vastly wider than that – important though the leakage aspect was – and a revealing story could be told of how it kept in touch with the whole Empire in connection with its security work on an international scale.

That side of its work, however, cannot be disclosed here, and, perhaps for very proper reasons, it never will be told. The sinews of the branches of the Security Intelligence Bureau were known to be stretched throughout the three armed services as well as in a wide civilian field, but very few were aware of the broader compass which it covered.

Full Story Yet to Come

MAJOR FOLKES has not yet told his story. If and when he does, it should equal any thriller. What will be the roles of Prime Minister Fraser and Minister of Works Semple must meantime remain a secret.

Perhaps, now that he is released from Army service and in semi-retirement, the late chief of the New Zealand Security Intelligence Bureau may write the full story of the 'Ross Fraud'.

I think he will – and no doubt he will give full details of the 'interviews' which he had with the Hon. H. G. R. Mason and Mr. Justice Cornish (then Solicitor-General) following the Ross case.

These interviews were ordered by the Prime Minister – in order, it is said, to compromise Folkes; but, if the remarks of Mr. Justice Cornish which were overheard in a passage of Parliament Buildings after the interviews are anything to go by, these legal luminaries signally failed in their purpose.

But of this, and much more, the full story must be awaited.

'CORPORAL'S' account of his interview with Major Kenneth Folkes, which is printed on pages 6 and 7, does not completely clarify the strange wartime story of the late Sidney Gordon Ross (alias 'Captain Calder'), who was kept under surveillance by the Security Intelligence Bureau for several months after he had allegedly disclosed an 'enemy plot' against the lives of the Prime Minister and the Hon. Robert Semple. After leaving New Zealand, Major Folkes performed important work in more active theatres of war, and is now back in England. According to the journalist who was commissioned by the OBSERVER to interview him there, he intends, at some future date, to tell the full story of the case as he saw it. In the meantime he has said sufficient to provide, in conjunction with what has gone before, the occasion for some further observations on the incidents which brought about his departure from New Zealand.

The main thing which emerges is that Major Folkes now confirms what was suspected all along, that the initiative in keeping a check on Ross, for the purpose of investigating his story, did not come from the Major at all, but from Messrs. Fraser and Semple, who, apparently, were completely hoaxed. Looking back, it seems scarcely credible that the Minister of Works should ever have taken seriously the fantastic tale that the Axis powers thought his removal desirable. From the evidence of his ministerial laxity, which was brought to light by the Turakina tunnel scandal, it might well be assumed that they would have been justified in desiring him to retain office for the longest possible time. However, such a viewpoint would obviously not appeal to Mr. Semple, whose bombastic election speeches reveal so colossal a vanity.

Major Folkes declares that he saw Ross only once, and then in company with Messrs. Fraser and Semple. In observing the traditional rule that a superior officer must not shelter behind his subordinates, the Major shows a keener perception of the proprieties than was displayed by those who did not hesitate to traduce him when it became politically expedient for them to 'run for cover'. The news that daily reports on the Ross case were handed to both Ministers, who saw no reason for ordering the Security Bureau to call off its dogs, provides an interesting sidelight on their conduct during the case. No one has ever flattered either of these politicians to the extent of regarding him as a paragon of valour. Today, therefore, sardonic merriment will arise over the recollection that, when brave New Zealanders were being killed and maimed overseas, two former anti-militarists were upset by the shocking thought that Hitler and Tojo were after them too.

Perhaps Major Folkes would be less grieved over his denouncement under cover of Parliamentary privilege if he were more familiar with the current routine practice of Socialist politicians in this Dominion. He will know that, in the hands of men of integrity, judgment and good faith, Parliamentary privilege is an indispensable weapon for the protection of the public. What he will not have learned from Westminster is that those who do not comprehend its true meaning and value, and lack the finer instincts, can and do degrade it to the level of the coward's basher. Here, then, Major Folkes is by no means alone in his complaint. Perhaps if he puts his full story into print, as he talks of doing, those who were at least equally culpable in the Ross–Calder case will again attack him from their places in Parliament. By then, however, their benches may be on the opposite side of the House.

Truth's report of Ross's death

New Zealand Truth
8 November 1946

DEATH OF
NOTORIOUS IMPOSTER

SYDNEY GORDON ROSS, con. man and thief, who spent almost half his 36 years in and out of gaol; who, in July of 1942, spoofed two Cabinet Ministers and the head of the Security Intelligence Bureau with a fantastic espionage story that cost the country a lot of money, is dead. He died recently in Green Lane (Auckland) chest clinic.

LOOKING back upon Ross's career, a life undistinguished by the spectacular in crime, but full of commonplace thefts, safe-breakings, and false pretences since he was 20, it is hard to understand how a man like Ross could fool anyone as completely as he did Major Kenneth Folkes, whom the Government imported as a super-counter-intelligence man for New Zealand's S.I.B.

Readers of 'Truth' well remember how Ross was given the name and rank of 'Captain Calder', unlimited spending money, a sleek American car, and headquarters at Rotorua's Grand Hotel to run to earth the phantom enemy agents who were plotting sabotage, invasion and what have you.

He spent three happy, carefree months at Rotorua, plus about £400 of the State's money entertaining some of the better people (who thought him 'rather charming').

In his more serious moments, and to justify lavish spending of the country's currency, he sent down to

Wellington hair-raising reports about the lairs and plots of Japanese and German under-cover men.

It fitted nicely into a pretty grim national picture, for at that time New Zealand was sending thousands of its men overseas, and the Dominion was dotted with road blocks, slit trenches and concrete shelters.

HOCUS-POCUS

As 'Captain Calder' Ross knitted a crazy patchwork of hocus-pocus that reputedly gave many a headache to the security sections of the three services, and cast a mantle of suspicion across the shoulders of innocent and unwitting citizens in different parts of the North Island. There was, of course, nothing to warrant that suspicion.

The two Cabinet Ministers who took up Ross's original tale must blush when they recall all this. They knew Ross for what he was – he confessed his criminal record – but accepted his condition that he would do nothing if the regular police force had anything to do with his 'investigations'.

He knew full well what would happen if the police cast a cold eye on the precious Mr. Ross and his cock-and-bull story. It happened when ultimately an odd fact came before their notice. Within two days they wiped the slate – and 'Captain Calder' – quite clean.

The men who did it were Superintendent (now Commissioner) J. Cummings, Detective-Sergeants J. Walsh, P.J. Nalder, E.A. Stevenson, J.A.White, A.H. Harding, Senior-Detective P. Doyle, Senior-Sergeant G.G. Kelly.

Ross confessed the whole affair was a gigantic hoax. 'Truth' exposed it.

After that Ross reverted to type. A few months later he was sentenced in Christchurch to a long term for false pretences, to which was added another nine months for escaping from Paparoa prison. Mr. E.C. Levvey, S.M., said at the time his alias should have been 'Baron Munchausen'. He was released on licence in January last, and soon afterwards went to Green Lane hospital chest clinic.

He died there, months later – a tall, slim crook who tried to bluff his way through life, but never thoroughly succeeded.

[Ross died on 6 November 1946]